50 Life Lessons

AF511999

50 Life Lessons

A Practical Guide
on How to **Maximise Happiness**

Suma Varughese

Foreword by
Brahma Kumari Shivani

HAY HOUSE

Hay House Publishers India
Australia • India
United Kingdom • United States

Hay House Publishers (India) Pvt. Ltd.
Muskaan Complex, Plot No.3, B-2 Vasant Kunj, New Delhi-110 070, India
Hay House Inc., PO Box 5100, Carlsbad, CA 92018-5100, USA
Hay House UK, Ltd., The Sixth Floor, Watson House, 54 Baker Street, W1U 7BU, UK
Hay House Australia Pty Ltd., 18/36 Ralph St., Alexandria NSW 2015, Australia

Email: contact@hayhouse.co.in
www.hayhouse.co.in

Copyright © 2022 Suma Varughese
Reprint 2023

The views and opinions expressed in this book are the author's own and the facts are as reported by her. They have been verified to the extent possible, and the publishers are not in any way liable for the same.

All rights reserved. No part of this publication may be reproduced, by any mechanical, photographic, or electronic process, or in the form of a phonographic recording, nor may it be stored in a retrieval system, transmitted, or otherwise be copied for public or private use – other than for 'fair use' as brief quotations embodied in articles and reviews – without prior written permission of the publisher.

ISBN 978-93-91067-71-7
ISBN 978-93-91067-72-4 (e-book)

Printed at Repro India Limited

I dedicate this book to the reader. The code of life is unbelievably hard to crack. And yet the key to a happy, healthy and successful life depends on it. If my book can help you understand and live life a little better than before, I would have nothing more to ask of it.

Contents

Foreword

At the outset, I congratulate Suma Varughese on bringing out yet another life-changing book. It is testimony to her unique skill, flair for writing, effort, and dedication. She shares her rich wisdom and experience in an elegant, loving, and practical way. Over the years, her work across various platforms has inspired individuals to embrace a positive lifestyle. I am certain that the book will start adding value to the lives of readers, the moment it finds its way into their hands.

Life is beautiful. If we can metaphorically say that the Planet is a playground, we are players in this 'Game of Life'. The ultimate purpose of this game being, winning our inner battles. As we gracefully make progress in this pursuit, our victory against the external odds and adversities becomes easier. We need to fix our gaze upon our own potential, keeping ourselves strong to overcome physical, emotional, mental and social barriers we meet along the way. Time and again, life tests our understanding, endurance, grit and passion. As in any other game, there are graded levels of difficulty in life – at times a child's play, so we ace it. At times it seems tough. We cannot figure out how to move forward or what life is attempting to teach us. We either falter, become disheartened, or even give up.

The book provides much-needed clarity on how to move forward when one feels stuck. Nevertheless, it is a valuable read even when life is smooth and perfect. Anyone who is keen to defeat barriers to success, such as stress, anger, irritation, insecurity, fear, or jealousy and live a meaningful life, will find this book handy. One can think of the book as a coach who helps us not only to 'play by the rules', but also enjoy the experience. A coach who can continuously think of what we as players might do and can do. A coach who shows us our potential and brings out our best. A coach who can sensitise us to the nuances, richness, ease, and complexity of life. And most importantly, a coach who constantly reminds us that nothing outside needs to be perfect for us to have a perfect inner state.

The pages ring true on a lot of elements, most of all, the idea that we have the power to create a glorious life. Whether or not we realise it, each of us is already equipped with all the tools to live more meaningfully, joyfully, and comfortably. We inherently or instinctively know right from wrong. How to value ourselves, how to practice kindness, how to respond to challenges, how to embrace changes, how to deal with suffering, how to handle difficult situations, how to create and sustain healthy habits, how to achieve goals.... it is a long list, but we actually have answers to them all. Every now and then we hear that inner voice guiding us. But today we are so caught up in the demands of everyday life, that we do not pause to listen to this innate wisdom. All we hear is the constant chatter of our cluttered minds. Overlooking what is essential, we engage in futile endeavours. This book takes us on a journey within. The spotlight is on the 'Self', because whether it is peace, happiness, success or respect that we seek – they are an inside job.

There are also times when we take life so seriously that we forget we are playing a game. So, our roles and responsibilities seem like a burden. We do not sit back to evaluate our performance. Performance evaluation needs a silent and calm mind. A mind that observes the scene from a detached perspective, to be able to see the bigger picture. Only then can we grasp the scenes of life objectively. The book helps to see the world through a different lens. It makes us ponder, question, and see ourselves, other people, our roles and relationships, career, goals, values, and even obstacles from a new perspective, one that is positive and optimistic.

The spiritual dimension of life woven in subtle, effective ways throughout the book is soul-nourishing. The book has captured life lessons that most of us seek to learn, and the values most of us agree upon. They reinforce the need to hold on to a compass of values to navigate through tough and easy times. The author's experience and wisdom are highlighted as a combination of biographical incidents, anecdotes, stories and quotes. The concise design, planning, structure, and narration encourage learning and contemplation. It is wise to learn from the mistakes of others than to commit them ourselves, after all. Dipping into this book even for 10 minutes can offer an enriching experience to a reader who can take away easy-to-implement guidelines and begin to 'win at life'.

—Brahma Kumari Shivani

Introduction

On June 27th, 2017, I turned 60. I was conscious that this was a milestone. In India, we have the tradition of calling the passage into the 60th year, the *shastipurthi*. Moreover, 60 usually augurs a passage into retirement in India. Either at 58 or 60, most people have to fold up their files, pull back their chairs and take leave of their labels, designations, salaries and so on. I, too, was doing likewise. The decision was not imposed upon me. I could have worked for another five years, but for a good many years before, I had pinpointed 60 as the right time to let go of my job and its attendant responsibilities and glories.

I rarely honour predetermined deadlines, for I believe in following the dictates of my inner guide. Yet, in this particular case both coincided, and around that time, I bid goodbye to *Life Positive*, a magazine I had nourished and nurtured for the last 21 years, but especially so in the last 12 years as its editor. It had been a faithful vessel to the mission I felt I had been set upon – to broadcast the vision of a New World, a world of peace, love, harmony and the brotherhood of man. A world that would orbit on the fulcrum of Oneness.

I had loved every moment of those 21 years. It was such a privilege to work for a magazine whose values coincided exactly with my own. How lucky I felt to be reading, researching and writing about subjects and activities that I was myself engaged in as a seeker, and to be meeting and interviewing kindred spirits. Most of all, it was a sacred honour to be doing work that would support readers on their own personal and spiritual journeys.

But all good things do come to an end and one is wise if one knows when one's time has come. I knew mine had. Moreover, a new path and a new dream were beckoning me, and I was eager to step on it. I had started holding writer's workshops a couple of years ago, and I found that I simply loved the process of teaching and being with people. The workshops were doing well, a proof that this was something I was meant to do.

So, there I was on the morning of my 60th year, delicately poised between what was, and what will be.

There was a sense of completion. I had reached my 60th year, no mean accomplishment for someone who had firmly believed that she would self-destruct at 40. My early life had been filled with so much confusion and unhappiness that I had drifted like a cork in a sea, with no will or volition of my own.

But the grace of the Divine had bestowed me with a spiritual awakening that had crystallised my amorphous being, and filled me with a deep understanding of life and how to lead it. The resultant insights transformed my life 360 degrees and, finally at 33, I took the reins of my life and moved purposefully ahead.

The next years were full of the painful yet meaningful task of changing myself bit by bit and becoming the person I was meant to be. The task is far from complete, but if I am in a state of relative equanimity, it is this awakening that I have to thank.

Thanks to it, I can look back at my 60 years and feel that my life on Planet Earth has not been a wasted one. I have contributed to the world. I have successfully handled my challenges. I have grown with every single day. I have expanded myself, and from being a fearful, limited, underconfident person, I have blossomed. I have successfully edited two magazines and earned the love and regard of thousands of readers. I have flowered into a confident speaker, a good leader, a wise counsellor and a loving daughter, sister, aunt and friend. I am living many of my dreams – doing the work I love, travelling to many places, increasingly relating to people with ease and love, and enjoying better health for some years. I am more and more comfortable within myself, and therefore more and more comfortable in the world.

I have grown as a person. I have learnt many lessons. Yes, not all. There is still so much to learn but I have learnt to be patient with my own self and to recognise that I am painting on the canvas of infinity, and if I do not succeed in the momentous task of learning it all in this lifetime, there are others.

It is against this background that the idea of this book suggested itself. There may be much to learn, but there is so much I have learnt. Could I share some of these lessons?

This seemed particularly apt given my understanding that life is one vast school and that we have taken incarnation in order to grow. The purpose of life is to grow as human beings, through learning the lessons that Life, our exacting but always loving school teacher, throws at us. This book then sums up my own growth graph on Planet Earth. The 50 life lessons I have shared here are the essence of all that I have learnt so far.

I hope that these lessons will support you, too, on your life's journey and hasten you towards the choicest gifts of life such as health, happiness, balance and peace.

Lesson #1

True Happiness Lies in the Happiness of the Other

I was 33 and miserable. I had been miserable for a long time. It had begun at the age of 16, when as a raw and unformed teenager, living in a tiny township in Orissa, I had been transported to the tony environment of Sophia College in Mumbai, the haunt of the upper classes.

I had not taken that transition well. My shaky self-esteem, my separation from family, my alienation from God (of which more later), my gawky awkwardness, all conspired to topple my equilibrium, and I slumped into a depression. The next 16 years went by in a daze. I was fearful, moody, reactive and insecure. Nothing interested me, nothing moved me. I had so little sense of self that when people talked to me, I often felt that there was no one there to respond or react to what they said. The words seemed to fall into a void without making even the slightest ripple. I had to struggle to paste on appropriate expressions on my otherwise expressionless face. I still remember that the publisher of *Beautiful*, the first magazine I had joined at 19 after having passed college, told some of my colleagues that he suspected I was on drugs. I was mortified, but how could I blame him, spaced out as I was?

I walked through life with a thick armour, afraid of getting too close to people lest they penetrate the emptiness behind it. I was always wrapped in a cloud of thoughts from which I could simply not emerge. I was in consequence absent-minded, forgetful and low on energy or drive. I drifted into journalism and into a succession of jobs within it, without much caring one way or the other. I was good at writing, and interested in people, so feature writing came easily to me. But I had not even a wisp of ambition to help me determine what my future should be, or what I should make of myself.

During my 20s, I clung to the familiar. While other friends were busy taking significant strides in their work, and personal lives by getting married and having kids, I clung fearfully to my jobs at the Sterling Newspaper, where I worked first as an assistant editor in a men's fashion quarterly, *GFQ*, and later at the more prestigious *Gentleman* magazine. I was petrified of relationships and was not interested in marriage. I shied away from any man who showed signs of interest in me. My life was completely on hold.

Then at 33, 1990 happened. It became not just the start of a new decade but, for me, the start of a whole new life. I felt as if life was determined to smoke me out of my lair. The first attempt was when I was unwittingly selected to join a newspaper in Dubai. I agreed to do so but chickened out at the last moment. That was only for starters. In a couple of months, I was given the post of editor of *Society* magazine, at that time, the only and original Page 3 magazine. It was a highly prestigious job and it came along with a certain public profile. I went into the editorship with dread in my heart because I was sure life had flushed me out and festooned me on top of the celebrity Christmas tree only in order to strike me down cruelly when it was proven that I could not deliver!

No sooner had I joined up than my life, thus far somnolent, began to go into overdrive. I was wrestling with the responsibilities of the job, the challenges of managing a team and, as if that was not enough, with an incipient relationship. I reluctantly became involved with someone, simply because he would not take no for an answer.

Confused, unhappy and totally unskilled at relationships, I blundered through it until, ultimately, the inevitable happened and he broke off the relationship. It was done in a dignified manner, which enabled me to receive two vital messages from him. One was that relationships were meant to be beautiful and ours had not been. The other was that I had not made him happy.

I have always been very sensitive to beauty. The idea that relationships could be beautiful was entirely new to me and captivated my imagination. What on earth was a beautiful relationship, I wondered, and longed to be able to experience it.

His complaint that I had not made him happy also went straight to my heart. Miserable as I had been for so many years, I had been thinking increasingly about happiness, and how it could possibly be found. Now, here was that word again!

I went home fearfully that night, for somewhere in my mind I had formed the firm conviction that being rejected in love would be the last straw for an already unstable mind, and I would topple into either insanity or death.

That night I had a dream of my late father leading me up a hillside. Somewhere, I felt him blessing me. The next morning I woke with a decision soldered on my soul. I was going to make that person happy no matter what it took. The moody will-o'-the-wisp that I was, I had no idea I was capable of making such an adamantine decision, but I knew that I was deadly serious, and that I would stop at nothing to achieve this.

The next few days were not easy. The person, who was still in my space, was being extremely nasty and aggressive. I was caught in a maelstrom of emotions – anger, jealousy, grief, frustration. I asked myself repeatedly how I was going to make him happy if I was boiling over all the time? After about four or five days of battling with these emotions, I had a moment of perfect clarity. I recognised that if I really wanted this person's happiness, then no matter what he said or did, I should be okay with it, because it was his happiness I wanted, not mine. If it made him happy to be angry, well then, let him rage till the cows came home. It would be sweet music to my ears because I wanted his happiness. If it made him happy to flirt with other women in my presence, well then, the more the merrier, for I was committed to supporting his happiness.

The moment it became clear to me that there was simply no conflict between what he wanted and what I wanted, and that I was okay for him to be exactly and absolutely as he was, I experienced my negative charge settling down and profound peace pervading me.

It was a seminal moment. A moment when my ego simply flipped out of me and I was free. The disappearance of the ego put me in touch with the real me. I remember the huge relief I felt when I touched base with my real Self. Thank goodness I was not the silly superficial person I thought I had been.

I soon converted this into a mantra. "*It is the other person's happiness that counts and not mine,*" I would say, and I would instantly transition out of my ego. It was almost a physical leap. I would feel myself settle midway between the other and me, thereby distancing me from my egoic world of thoughts, feelings, likes, dislikes, wants, aversions and so on. In that space, I could arbitrate between the other and me with faultless objectivity. It was a profound experience to be so liberated from the pulls and pressures of one's emotional, psychological and physical needs. No matter what anyone said or did, the chanting of the mantra would cause the initial reaction to recede, and leave me in a state of radiant peace. No one and nothing could disturb me. In that space, I was totally free of the other. I have had someone verbally abuse me, and not stir a hair.

All this happened more than 29 years ago, but I recall it as freshly as if it happened yesterday. And why not? It was, quite simply, the most momentous experience of my life. Within a month I was able to put together the jigsaw puzzle of life. The more I was actively prioritising the happiness of the other, the happier I was getting. I realised that I had opened a conduit to inexhaustible happiness. In order to secure my happiness, all I had to do was draw happiness from the happiness of everyone around me and strive actively to reduce their misery. Happiness, I discovered, was not a direct route. It was deflected from the happiness of the other. And all this while I had been obsessed with finding personal happiness. I had been looking for happiness where it could not be found.

This, I recognised with a sense of electric excitement running through me, was the design of life. We were meant to get our happiness from the happiness of the other.

And if there was a design, there had to be a designer. In that instant, my relationship with the Divine, ruptured at the age of 14, was once again revived, and I felt myself expanding with a vast relief. How good it felt to go back to God. It was not until I lost God that I realised how vital Her existence was for me. I suspect that my depression was caused partially by the absence of God in my life.

I also realised that if we are meant to get our happiness from the happiness of the other, then we are connected and not separated, as we mistakenly believe. And that put me in direct touch with the Vedantic truth of Oneness.

Putting these truths together, I recognised that the most important thing in the world was to prioritise happiness and not the other goals that consume our lives such as money, fame, power and the endless pursuit of possessions. These were not where happiness lay. On the contrary, they distracted us from our true pursuit.

It did not take me long to discern the purpose of life. Prioritising other people's happiness was hard work. It took effort to go beyond the ego, to push oneself to be there for the other, to transcend the hurt and give the other the space to be hurtful. Each time I achieved this, I felt myself getting stronger. And that ultimately became the purpose of life. To grow. To become more patient, more loving, more courageous, wiser, more focussed – in short, more of everything positive. We were meant to grow as human beings. Mind you, at that time, I had no idea about the karmic theory or about enlightenment. I had no idea that our ultimate purpose was to achieve Godhood, but this I knew. Grow we must!

All in all, I felt that the whole design of life had been revealed to me. How to live, what to prioritise, what to free myself of, what to move towards. The keys to my life and to life itself had been given to me, and I was finally ready to live.

In that heady one month, I also pieced together my own individual purpose of life. It was to help heal the world of its misery. I had been miserable for so long that the incandescent happiness that now flooded me felt unbelievably good. And there was misery everywhere. All around me people were locked in conflicts with themselves, others, life and God. I had learnt how to free myself of conflicts. Could I not help others do so, too? Of course, it was a very broad statement and I had no idea how I was going to execute it, but to heal the world of its misery, as far as I could, was what I was meant to do. I had simply no doubt about it.

And indeed, looking back, everything I did thereafter has had that as its intent. Every article I have written after leaving Magna Publishing in 1996, and joining *Life Positive*, has been with the idea of spreading awareness of a higher and more holistic way of life, of guiding, supporting and inspiring people to work on themselves, to shift perspectives and to heal. My workshops, too, though ostensibly on writing, have helped people heal from fears and self-doubt and filled them with confidence and inspiration, for they are founded on spiritual principles.

I have dealt with this experience in some detail, because not only is this the most significant life lesson I have received, but almost all my other life lessons in one way or other, hinge on it.

Lesson #2

The Purpose of Life Is Growth

I was an avid reader all my life, but rarely did I come across any writer who was able to state forthrightly and unambiguously what life was, and what its purpose was. In fact, all of them skittered around the subject and, more often than not, declared that these big questions had no answer.

Fortunately, as I mentioned in my earlier chapter, my spiritual awakening helped me understand that the purpose of life was growth. Later, after I had begun to read up on spirituality and encountered the magic word, enlightenment, it became easier to understand why growth was our common purpose. We can only get enlightened when we grow as human beings to a point where we have healed ourselves fully from our wounds and conditioning. This also means that we will have grown prodigiously in strength, capability, acceptance and inner power. When our ego dissolves and disappears, our job is done, because then there is nothing to stop us from uniting with the Divine Source, whom we were always a part of. Only ongoing growth by using all of life's circumstances as an instrument for it will equip us for the divine union.

Knowing that growth is the purpose of life not only enables us to strive for enlightenment, but also fine-tunes our approach to the journey itself.

Once we recognise that every situation and circumstance in our life is set up for our growth, and life on Planet Earth is one vast school, it transforms and clarifies our outlook on life remarkably.

Where earlier I used to dread and fear the problems life inevitably deposited on my plate, I now know that fate, far from being a malevolent agency that delights in making me squirm, is actually a loving teacher, determined to get me to expand my horizons and break through my barriers. Fate or life or God is incapable of giving up on us. It will give us the same problem over and over again – perhaps troublesome relationships, poverty or poor health – until we confront and learn to overcome it. Mostly, this calls for us to introspect, see what we are doing wrong and take corrective steps. When this happens, not only will our problem melt away, but we will experience a surge of strength, confidence and capability that will move us one tiny fraction ahead of where we were.

To see life as an instrument of growth shifted my relationship with it altogether. Instead of being dragged kicking and screaming through life, I now found myself cooperating with it, after the initial gnashing of teeth and smiting of breasts.

Once I began to understand the law of karma, I developed a more refined perception of life and the importance of growth. Ultimately, it was not God or fate who gave us the problem. We ourselves had created them through our thoughts, words and actions, either in this life or another. No one else was responsible. This made it even easier to accept the events that befell me. It was pointless blaming the agency through which an event had happened, such as the boyfriend who had ditched me, or the health issues that cropped up. My own actions, either in this lifetime or the past, had put me in this position. My job was to patiently bear the event instead of breaking into reaction, and through wise action and self-restraint, resolve the situation; eventually emerging the wiser for having gone through it.

This knowledge has given me the wisdom to deal correctly with life and therefore, more often than not, extricate myself gracefully from situations. Of all problems, it is perhaps relationships that have the greatest power to plunge us into despair and hopelessness. Every day around me, I see men and women caught in the coils of incompatible relationships, or at loggerheads with parents, children, colleagues and siblings. Everywhere, the ego has us in its thrall. Their suffering is immense.

I, too, have had my share of contentious relationships. Knowing that life is about growth gives me the impetus to use these conflicts to accelerate my evolution. I have learnt to take responsibility for the situation. Where did I go wrong? What did I do to exacerbate the situation? Even in cases when the other person seems clearly in the wrong, if I go far enough, I can always trace an interaction where I might have reacted in anger, or was judgemental, insensitive to their feelings or ignored them. I have found that the moment I discover my responsibility in the matter, my anger against the other collapses and I can set about making amends such as apologising, and building bridges. Very few relationships have collapsed because I salvage them through a willingness to acknowledge my faults and a real commitment to the relationship. If the other is intractable and insists on rupturing the relationship, I let it be, knowing that in the fullness of time we will come together again, if we are meant to. I try very hard not to write off relationships, unless, of course, I am subjected to unacceptable behaviour.

Similarly, I have been assailed by many health challenges. Most of these I trace to a highly emotional temperament, a weakness for food and a rather traumatic deconditioning journey that forced me to confront my many weaknesses. I am clear, therefore, that the illnesses are karmic retribution and have to be received in that light. So, I try my best to grow through them.

For instance, when I was diagnosed with a mild case of asthma hinging on allergy to wheat and dairy, I was filled with a wild fear. I knew that my addiction to food had brought me to this pass, but I also knew that I did not have the self-control to steer clear of forbidden food. It brought to the head my hopeless bond to food and made me determined to work on it. My ayurvedic doctor had imposed a stiff diet upon me which not only forced me to eschew wheat and wheat products, milk and milk products but also most fruits, all gas-giving vegetables and all pulses save *mung dal*. This was my first attempt to discipline my wayward food habits. It was hard. I felt sorry for myself very often when I saw others wolfing down what was barred to me. When I passed bakeries and breathed in the aroma of fresh bread, my heart clenched. Imagine not being able to eat sandwiches and biscuits anymore! How on earth would I manage my in-between meals munching? Slowly, though, the brakes came on. It was easier for me to resist tempting morsels. My hand no longer went swiftly to convey a tasty morsel to my mouth before reason could kick in. I still gave in to temptation, but far less than before.

Best of all, I was adapting to my regimen and making peace with all that was forbidden to me. I began to experiment with alternative *rotis* made of ragi, rice or bajra. I began to relish making tasty dishes out of gourds like pumpkin, ridge gourd and *louki*. l freed myself of the habit of munching something in the evening by having dinner as soon as I reached home from work. And slowly, I developed what was actually a healthy diet regimen that not only kept me relatively healthy but also relatively slim.

A few years later, once again karma kicked in and I was diagnosed with Irritable Bowel Syndrome, which manifested as severe constipation, bloating and so on. Once again, terrible fear and anxiety gripped me as I confronted the consequences of my inability to control what I ate. Not just fear, but guilt and shame, too. My lack of self-control diminished me in my own eyes and deeply affected my self-esteem.

This time, I was aware that the lessons I was meant to learn went beyond the physical. The IBS was also here to flush out my negative emotions and heal me of them. It has been a long journey and not fully over, but for the last couple of years, I have progressed hugely in going beyond my negative feelings. Not only have the feelings substantially reduced, but I no longer identify with them as much. They are not me, after all.

I know within myself that I am essentially absolutely healthy because that is my true nature. And I also know that at the subconscious level I have set up these illnesses as a safeguard against my low self-control when it comes to food. The day I can trust myself to turn down the most tempting morsel if it is not in my best interest, will be the day I return to rude health.

My constant endeavour is to grow through all that confronts me in all areas of life. And it has transformed me as a person and how I view life. It is quite simply, one of the most potent mantras for life.

Lesson #3

You Can Change Yourself

This truth may seem self-evident in today's times because there is so much literature on self-healing, self-transformation and the innate flexibility of the brain.

But it never hurts to repeat it. No matter how far gone you are, you can change. If there is anything that my life is a testimony to, it is this truth.

When I think of the person I was before my awakening sent me hurtling into self-transformation, I catch my breath with wonder. Was that passive, unhappy, confused, touchy, regressive, clueless, fearful person really me? Today, I feel I have shucked off most of these epithets, though I still have a way to go with passivity and absentmindedness. I have made a pretty thorough overhaul of myself, and would consider myself to be purposeful, passionate, caring, positive, enthusiastic, courageous, loving, giving, a visionary, someone who never gives up, does not shirk challenges and has a very good understanding of life and how to live it

I remember, though, that when I started out on the path to change, I only had my inner voice to guide me. The available literature of that time (1992-94) decreed that after the age of 30, it was almost impossible to change. Our personality was virtually cast in stone by then, it was believed, and the grooves in the brain had been set. It was dismaying to be going against the laws of science, but undeterred, I forged on, for I was determined that even if I died in the process,

I would attain the happiness I had experienced for the one year that the awakening lasted.

So, I speak from experience when I say that you can change. Do you have a bad temper? You can heal it and become as sunny-natured as the next person. Do you consider yourself to be lazy, a spendthrift, a liar, a thief, an addict, a philanderer and so on? No matter. You can change.

Take heart from the stories in our mythologies. Remember Angulimala, thus called because of the fearsome garland of fingers wrested from the hands of his murdered victims that he wore around his neck? He had vowed to get a thousand fingers into his garland and was on his way to accomplishing this task when he met the Buddha. Unlike the terrified populace that was quaking behind closed doors, the Buddha smiled at him serenely, unafraid and loving. Shocked and baffled by the Buddha's reaction that completely deprived him of the power he was accustomed to wield over the other, Angulimala paused. And then came the transformation. Slowly, the Buddha's unconditional love and acceptance won him over, and he eventually became one of his principal disciples.

Or take the case of Valmiki, who was once a fearsome bandit called Ratnakar. When he tried to hold up Narad Muni, the sage asked him if his family was willing to take part in his bad karma that robbing and stealing from others was earning him. When his family refused to do so, it was a turning point for Ratnakar who thereafter became Valmiki, the writer of the Ramayana. As they say, every sinner has a future, and every saint a past.

Before my awakening, I had written myself off. I was deeply disappointed in the person I had proved to be. I could find no merit in myself and had no faith in my capacity to lead my life. But the awakening proved to me that God had not written me off. God believed in me even if I had not believed in myself. God believed I could change, else She would not have given me the awakening.

This was the one truth that kept me going through the agonisingly long journey of self-change. Because while change is possible, change also takes time. I really do not believe in the airy-fairy belief that you can change deep-rooted habits, belief systems and behavioural patterns in 21 days. Personally, any change has taken me decades; my own experience is that innumerable layers have to unpeel before one can confidently say one has transcended one's weaknesses. But the great hope is that one is not condemned to one's nature or personality. As someone eloquently put it, biology is not destiny. And the journey itself is so meaningful.

So how does change happen? There are many spiritual tools and techniques to support growth, such as meditation, yoga, the Buddhist eight-fold path, jnana yoga, bhakti yoga, karma yoga, raja yoga and a million other routes. No matter the route, inner change pivots around two aspects: awareness and acceptance. You can only change what you are aware of, and you can only change when you accept it.

That is all. Change does not happen by vowing to change. Or by willpower and determination. It is a happening that slowly manifests. It is a natural phenomenon, like a flower blooming or a fruit ripening. It is not in your hands. It is in the hands of the Universe. But you can facilitate it by peaceful awareness and acceptance. One more tool that works very well is affirmation. This counters the almost non-stop barrage of negative self-talk we unconsciously download upon ourselves.

Yet another thought that can help with self-change is the recognition that, ultimately, we are aspects of God, and therefore we are all the good things that we long to be, and none of the bad things that we fear we are. So, don't pay too much attention to the things you don't like about yourself, and keep endorsing all the things that you actually are.

Another thing. Just as you have the mandate to change, so does everyone else. Do not condemn people with your tightly held judgements. Do not say or even think that they are incapable of change. For the tender psyche can often wilt and die in an inhospitable environment. Tell a person often enough that he cannot change, and he loses heart and writes himself off. The reverse is also true. Believe in the other's potential for change and he may well redeem himself. Such faith is the best gift we can give another.

Lesson #4

Life Is Perfect

This isn't an easy one to get. And it took me ages, *ages*, to not just figure this out but to accept it even nominally.

When you look around you or even within you, the last thing you see is perfection. Because what we mistake for perfection is a life where all problems are solved, we are in a constant state of happiness, life always goes our way, and nothing ever disturbs our equanimity.

Our idea of perfection is not just unrealistic but undesirable. It has the static quality of dead things. I often look at gardens manicured to perfection, and I find them dull when I compare them to the wilderness crafted by Nature, teeming with growth, leaves and branches shooting off in all directions. It may have no apparent regard for proportion and harmony, but what a riot of untrammelled life.

I remember I had a hostel mate in college whose one great beauty was her thick shiny coat of hair that fell to her waist like a glistening waterfall. The girl was so in thrall to her hair that she used to walk ramrod stiff, so that her hair would always fall in the same straight line. Eventually, the very regularity of the hair lost its sheen for me. Other hostel mates had hair that may not have been as thick or shiny, but they were so much more alive, as their hair bounced around their faces, blew in the wind or escaped charmingly from a ponytail in wayward tendrils.

Stasis, sameness, regularity, predictability – all these are inimical to life. Life is dynamic, spontaneous, unpredictable and uncontrollable. Instead of bridling and taming it to suit our tastes, can we leap bareback upon it and pelt along?

By this I mean that can we learn to take life as it comes? So the cake that we baked sank. Can we make a trifle pudding with it? The boy we loved fell in love with our best friend instead. Heartbreaking as it is, can we at some point take our life back instead of making it a graveyard from that day onwards? Fine, we did not get admission to an IIT or to a foreign university, but can we use that opportunity to evaluate our options? A friend swotted really hard to get into the IAS. He did not make the cut, but the hard work he put in for his UPSC exams enabled him to crack the banking exam and get a job with a premier Indian bank. Another friend could not realise her cherished dream of becoming a pilot because of faulty vision, but today is an ace IT executive.

We cannot control life; we can only move in tandem with it. And that very dynamism is its biggest charm. Once we know that, we will cease to judge and label life, and learn to dance with it. And then we will see life as perfect in its imperfection. Troubles become zestful challenges, problems become puzzles that can help us order our lives better, relationship problems help us understand others and ourselves better. And life becomes a vast learning laboratory.

The innate perfection in the design of life manifests even more as we grow old enough to see how the random events strewn across our lives have actually been knitted together to form a cohesive pattern. Vikas Khanna, the well-known chef, had a bad leg that prevented him from playing with other kids during his childhood days. Instead, he spent time helping his grandmother in the kitchen. What a perfect break for one destined to be a chef! It is really true that our most gruelling hardships become the source of our greatest strength and power. In my own case, I went through a low-grade chronic depression from the age of 16 to the age of 33. Those years were dark, muffled and cold. If someone had told me that something marvellous would come out of it, I would have laughed (though quite frankly, there were periods when I simply could not laugh).

What brought me out of the depression was my spiritual awakening. From the depths of confusion and misery, I was elevated to a pristine understanding of life and how to live it, as well as a rock-solid experience of happiness.

Would I have had this awakening had I not been so miserable for so long? I wonder, for it was unhappiness that set me actively searching for happiness, and definitely helped trigger the experience. If I had not been miserable, would happiness have meant that much to me? I don't think so. I felt as if I had taken a PhD in misery. I knew that state of mind intimately. I knew what triggered it. I knew how it felt in all its avatars. And it made me deeply empathetic to unhappy people everywhere. I understood them. I felt a kinship with them, and I longed to help them in just the same way the Universe had helped me.

So, yes, I am deeply grateful for my depression, for it has made me who I am today.

Life is perfect in yet another way, and that is that we draw circumstances into our lives that are ideal for our level of evolution. The Universe is always constructing stage sets to help us master lessons, void karma and get to the next level. I remember that when I first started working on healing myself of my conditioning, I was completely low on energy and could scarcely cope with difficulties. The benevolent Universe literally built a scaffolding around me that protected me from almost all challenging situations or people. The first two years at *Life Positive* required me to work from home, so I felt as if a little haven was created for me where I only had to interact with loved ones. Two years later, I felt ready to step out. In tandem with that thought, my company took an office in Nariman Point and we began to recruit a skeleton staff. By the end of 2004, I could feel the last of the scaffolding being taken away as life pushed me into many challenges.

My sister fell ill, and I had to take care of her. Simultaneously, I also agreed to take over as editor *of Life Positive*, which brought in its wake many relationship struggles. Clearly, the Universe now deemed me ready to take on life at any level. After 2004, there followed many difficult circumstances that were designed to help me discharge the karmas I had accumulated like contracting asthma, and having my mother bedridden for two-and-a-half years as a paralytic.

A third way perfection is imbedded in imperfection is that even when things don't go according to plan, sooner or later we will find that we were denied something only because something even better is coming our way. I have noticed this time and again. For instance, when I was applying for visas to the US, Canada and England in 2017, my agent first applied for Canada, then England and got around to the US only a few weeks before my departure. I was annoyed by it, but later found that it was probably best so, because in the interim, PM Narendra Modi had visited the US and President Trump had since relaxed his rules on visiting the US. Perhaps if we had applied earlier, I might not have got the visa.

So, be of stout heart. There is purpose and meaning in everything that comes our way. Knowing this makes it so much easier to accept life and inch towards surrender.

Lesson #5

God Exists

To the believer, everything, even the tiniest twig, sings of God's existence. To him or her, God's existence is manifest in all that lives, in the astonishing order of the Universe, in the colours that surround us, in the miracle of the human body, in the beauty of our wonderful planet and in the love that shines through the eyes of a dog. To the non-believer, the chaos, injustice, unhappiness and suffering all around is a clear testimony of the absence of God.

I have been on both sides of the equation, and I believe that this may be a process for many of us. Scott L. Peck, author of *The Road Less Travelled*, wisely wrote that in the journey towards God, you often progress from blind belief to atheism and only then do you forge a direct relationship with Divinity.

I was 14 when I stopped believing in God. At school, I had been exposed to Darwin's theory of evolution and, unsurprisingly, I found it hard to reconcile it with the Biblical notion that God made the world in six days and rested on the seventh.

It was not easy to give up God. I came from a family of devout Christians and the idea of not believing in God was blasphemy. For days I wondered if I would be struck with lightning, but nothing happened and I was left alone with my disbelief. I have to admit, I missed God. I often tried returning to Her by praying, but there was no answering echo, no sense of being heard – the line had gone dead. And yet, when I saw people like my mother or my friend Maria, so ardent and firm in their faith, I deeply envied them. I knew they had something I lacked – a fulcrum on which their lives revolved, a source of strength and support that was denied to me. Their personalities, too, had a radiance, a power, a certainty that I longed for. They seemed to know exactly what to do in all circumstances and situations, while I vacillated endlessly, never able to make up my mind about anything at all.

My 16 years of godlessness were a confused and unhappy time for me. I understood nothing about life, I seemed to have no parameter against which to make decisions; my inner radar was missing. I was hopelessly lost and I knew it. Fortunately, my spiritual awakening catapulted me to a whole new level. Best of all, I was able to go back to God in a way that worked for me – rationally, with a logic that I could buy (see Lesson #2).

I cannot tell you of the relief and joy that flooded me when I took back my relationship with God. And that is not surprising because I later discovered that I am truly a lover of God. I am a *bhakta*, someone to whom the presence of God is almost a physical necessity, as much as the air to breathe, or the water to drink. Now that I knew God existed, my world began to right itself and I, too, like the ones I envied earlier, had a fulcrum or a centre to operate from. That centre was the sure knowledge that God existed, believed in me and was willing me to succeed in the game of life. I was not alone in the bewildering sea.

Studying and understanding God became a passion for me. Who exactly was this being? Thanks to the fact that I had attained my awakening through as secular a reason as a love affair, I had transcended religion. Therefore, God was not equated in my mind with Jesus Christ. Indeed, I was quite clear that restricting God to a personage was to constrict God. My God was nameless and formless. Study of Hindu philosophy and the Vedas introduced me to the concept of Brahman, which I identified with deeply. I also deeply resonated with the Vedic concept of Oneness, in which the Creator and creation were One. What a lofty, thrilling concept. Imagine, the Creator permeating all of Creation, therefore rendering even the tiniest clod of clay holy! And what is more, if Oneness with the Creator was the fundamental truth of life, then we were all connected. We lived in an interconnected world.

My imagination was fired with the idea of how we would live in a world of interconnection and innate sacredness. Our ancient Indian culture gives us many pointers to this question because it has been designed on spiritual lines. All the old systems are based on Oneness. Thus, education equipped the child with the means not just of leading a life but also to eventually strive for enlightenment; healing through Ayurveda and Siddha emphasised the connection between the body, mind and spirit. Architecture through Vastu Shastra helped us to align with the larger cosmos, while the predictive science of astrology was based on the position of the sun, moon and stars.

But there are even more implications. How would Oneness regulate our social lives? What kind of economic and social systems would it create? To my mind, an experiential understanding of Oneness will also enable us to lead ethical lives. In an interconnected world, causing misery to another is tantamount to causing ourselves misery. Therefore, our focus will be on supporting others in their lives because only that will secure our own well-being. The concept of Oneness would help politicians serve the public instead of feathering their own nests, it would help corporates factor in interests of the environment before drawing up their plans, and it would prevent the common man from abusing public property or in abusing the system for personal profit.

In an interconnected world, only focussing on the larger good will secure our own good.

Seeing everything as sacred has long been the Indian way of life. Flowers, trees, cows, rivers and mountains have always been regarded as sacred. If we can take this logic further and actively see everything and everyone as sacred, all the societal divisions based on caste, community, colour, creed and species will melt away. Everything and everyone has the right to exist because they have been given life by God, and they are part of Creation. The beautiful concept of the One-world Family, where we all live as members of one giant family, may actually come about.

Thus, a proper understanding of God's nature can help us create a world that is an extension of God.

But, of course, there are other conundrums that atheists point to when it comes to God. What about the monstrous suffering that our world is ridden with? How can we believe in a God who allows innocent children to be abused and killed, or that allowed a Hitler or a Pol Pot to exist? Only knowledge of karma and reincarnation can fully answer this query. Annie Besant, the well-known President of the Theosophical Society, asked this very same anguished question when her infant son kept falling grievously ill. It was the exposure to the concepts of karma and reincarnation that threw light on the question. Her son had lived before, not just once but many times, and his illness was the karmic consequence of his deeds in an earlier life. Karma tells us that we and only we are responsible for our suffering, which we draw through our thoughts, words and actions. The Buddha says it strikingly, "Suffering follows an evil thought like the wheels of a cart follow the oxen that drive it."

Our every thought, word and deed has consequences and not all of these consequences can visit us in this lifetime. This, therefore, brings us to reincarnation. The cycle of birth and death is activated by our karmas. We are forced to take repeated birth in order to expiate our karmas. (For more details on the subject, see Lesson #23)

God has created no suffering on Planet Earth. It is we who have created misery for ourselves and others, through our misguided thoughts, words and actions. Moreover, God never punishes us. She has set into motion the impersonal law of karma that metes out to us the perfect justice that is our due. Nor should we ever imagine karma to be a punitive force. Let us remember that we take incarnation on Planet Earth lifetime after lifetime, without having a clue as to what we are doing here, or where we came from or where we are headed. Most of us go to our deaths not much the wiser. We are therefore bound to make mistakes. And since God has given us freedom of will, we are entitled to make these mistakes. But in order to learn from our mistakes and not wallow in them ad infinitum, the corrective agency of karma gives us some gentle and not-so-gentle reminders.

God stands separate from karma, willing us to succeed in the game of life. And what is this game? According to the Indian philosophy, Creation is nothing but God's play, a *lila*. In order to experience Herself in multitudinous ways, the One became many. Thus, all of us enter Planet Earth thinking that we are individual beings, when we are actually part of the One. The game is to see through all the illusions woven around us and to return to Godhead. When we achieve that unity with the Divine, we wake up permanently from the dream of separation.

When you consider how extremely challenging life on Planet Earth can often be, it may seem like a cruel joke to send us here for play, but then again, who can deny that the game is fascinating and, as gruelling as life on earth can be, it is equally rewarding, beautiful and exciting. The proof of this is that few of us want to die.

The closer we get to God, the more dazzling appears this Being. For one thing, Her creativity is endless and profound.

The whole Universe is a staggering display of God's ability to create. Just look at the multitude of human beings, each different from the other. How astonishing. Ever studied the leaves of different trees, the flowers from diverse plants or the array of fruits? The sunrises and sunsets? What a feast of variety, beauty and colour is laid before us. The more you delve into any aspect of nature, the more awe-inspiring God appears. Look at the perfection of the human body. The orderly way the planets rotate around the sun. The succession of days and nights, the blending of one season into another, or nature's self-sustaining cycles such as creating life out of soil and returning each life back to soil.

We can never hope to understand God fully, but studying God increases our capacity to wonder at and worship this personage, and to love and be grateful to Her. How does God create? Personally, it seems that creation happens through God simply through intention. As the Bible says, "I Am the Alpha and the Omega." Just like God set the law of karma into motion, She set evolution into motion. Creation flows through God so copiously and profoundly simply because of the nature of God.

And to think we are a part of this Being. Can any words be enough to praise Her nature?

Best of all, despite the riot of colours and lives and forms that our world is full of, God Herself is nowhere to be found. There is no ownership of anything, no vainglorious showing off, nothing. Only Creation carries the signature of God and gives us glimpses of Her nature.

What moves me most about God is Her willingness to give us freedom of will. Such is Her trust in us, She is willing to risk our destroying the planet wantonly, as we have often done before and which we seem in imminent danger of doing yet again. Moreover, God does not even want us to obey or love Her. She wants us to look for and find Her when we are ready to do so, and surrender willingly to Her.

God does not believe in force and coercion. How great is our God!

Surely only love can enable someone to do this? God is love. Deep, unconditional and absolute love. And love again is resonant in all of Creation. It is love that causes the trees to flower and fruit for the sake of others, and makes the leaves fall to the ground in autumn, and motivates the rain to fertilise the soil and plants to yield up their produce. Love, sacrifice and generosity run like a golden thread through all of Creation and reflect the nature of God.

I also absolutely know that God is so expansive and vast a Being that She accepts and forgives everything that we do. Yes, there are consequences to what we do and karma takes care of that, but God herself will never reject us or punish us. Her love is constant. Every time you fail to feel God's presence in your life, take it as a given that you have moved away from God, and not the reverse.

What a privilege to be part of such a Being. What a lodestar for us to aspire to. What a gift to have such endless potential available to us as part of Creation. There is meaning, magic and wonder in a life permeated by God. As it says in the Bible, God is the way to everlasting life. I hope that you, like me, will quickly find an authentic way to connect with this Power.

Lesson #6

Inner Change Is a Happening

I suspect most of us would not enter the spiritual path if we had any inkling how long it would take us to get enlightened. In its initial stages, my own journey had been so internalised and so devoid of external guidance (to be frank, I had no idea that I was a seeker, or that there was a whole movement out there. I thought I was the sole discoverer of all these truths, and I wondered if perhaps I would become a second Jesus Christ!), that I had no option but to follow the promptings of my inner guide. My first experience of inner work was when I stumbled upon the realisation that I was whole and perfect, and that the faulty personality I had so far considered to be me was only a construct of conditioning. Forthwith, I began chanting, "I am whole and perfect" constantly and, within four months, my heart chakra opened up (I have described the experience in more detail in Lesson #31). This convinced me that four months was all it would take for me to free myself of my conditioning, and therefore it was with great insouciance that I set off to heal myself.

What's more, I gave my colleagues at *Society* notice that I would soon be unveiling a dazzling vision of the magazine. My colleagues waited. And waited. I, on the other hand, was becoming increasingly alarmed. Months were piling up and, still, the inner change had not happened. When the months became a year and even more, I recognised that my timeline had better change.

In a stroke of wisdom, I realised that the changes I was crafting into my system were meant not just for a lifetime, but for eternity, for we carry only two things with us: our psyche or character which is the sum total of the work we have done on ourselves, and our relationships.

I asked myself that if I was working against the background of eternity, should I really quibble if inner change took a few more years? I remember even jokingly remarking to a friend that I was okay to dodder up the enlightenment path at 60. Ironically, I am past 60 and that magic moment of inner transformation is still to come!

However, what this realisation did do for me is that I stopped trying to rush my inner growth. Everyone knows that you can't rush it, but by trying to force it, you can slow it down even more. Remember that Zen story about an ardent young monk who went to a Zen master and asked him how long it would take him to get enlightened? The Zen master replied that it would take 10 years. "What if I were to meditate day and night?" asked the monk, eagerly. "In that case," said the Master calmly, "it will take you 20 years."

So, I consented to allow change to happen at its own pace, even though my inner state felt so conflicted that I could hardly stand it. The gulf between the person I was showing up to be, now that my consciousness had exploded my shadow self into the full light of awareness, was excruciatingly far from the person I longed to be, or indeed was, in the very depth of my being.

Slowly, the awareness of working against a background of eternity seeped into me and influenced me. I realised that in the seeking game there were no deadlines to meet, no targets to achieve, no competition to beat. I simply had to do my best, moment to moment, and that was all that was asked of me. God did not want me to achieve enlightenment overnight. He wanted it to happen when it was meant to happen. I was meant to evolve at the same imperceptible slow pace that a flower blossomed or a fruit ripened.

Meanwhile, around me, people were still pelting down the path at an unbelievable pace. They were keen as mustard to change others, to change society, to bring about the 100th monkey phenomenon. There is no time to be lost, they breathed impatiently. It is now or never. I know friends who have committed to transforming a billion people, healing Planet Earth by the year 2022 and so on.

Such talk today leaves me completely unmoved. I am convinced that goals like these are set by the ego, which adores ambitious goals and the glory of achieving them. I, on the other hand, agree with Ramakrishna Paramahansa when he profoundly observed that it is God who is running the world and not we. Whether or not we do anything about it, the cosmos will still function peacefully, patiently and harmoniously in accordance with the larger design. We are not indispensable. God is sufficient for all things. All we can do is humbly contribute, without dragging in the ego's need for self-aggrandisement.

Let us not be in a hurry to bring in the Spiritual Age, free the world of patriarchal energy or heal the world. Everything will happen when it is meant to happen, whether we do anything about it or not. However, our hurry and our impatience can drag it down, for in our hurry we will act wrongly and without wisdom.

Hurry tends to hijack the agenda, to think short-term, to react in a knee-jerk manner, to not see the big picture. Stepping aside, keeping the framework of eternity, freeing ourselves of doer-ship and doing what comes to us without imposing deadlines will enable us to contribute to the best of our capacity.

Above all, let us work on ourselves. This is the single most powerful thing we can do to bring about the Spiritual Age. Working on ourselves patiently, unflaggingly and without hurry; who knows what incredible things we may achieve without even knowing it!

Lesson #7

Nothing Is a Big Deal

As someone who had a perilously low opinion of her capabilities and ability to cope with life, any problem towered over me like a Colossus. For the larger part of my life, I lived in a state of near panic, absolutely sure that I would mess up anything that could be messed up.

So just about everything was a very big deal. Fear had a near-total grip over me. Through it all, I kept up my inner work – my affirmations about being whole, perfect and complete, my awareness of my inner feelings and thoughts and my strife to accept them. (The last one was often extremely difficult. It usually ended in my affirming that I could not accept what I could not accept. But even that gave me some expansive room.) And the feelings slowly diffused. Yet they were far from gone, and one sure way of bringing them surging to the surface was any illness that confronted me.

This was particularly true when I came down with Irritable Bowel Syndrome. Months and even a year passed without the problem getting resolved, making me more and more despondent. Finally, I went to a homoeopath and was given some medicine. I had been strictly warned to jettison all other medicines. But without medicines, I was unable to void my bowels, and I was warned that it would take a few days before the homoeopathy medicines kicked in. I harangued the homoeopath every day asking permission to take a laxative until, one day, she belted into me, "We have patients who have been unable to void their bowels for a month; at least you are not so bad. You please do what I tell you."

After I put down the phone, I felt strangely comforted. Maybe my illness was not such a big deal, after all. Maybe I had built it up too much in my head? I remember sitting in front of the TV, feeling tranquil and peaceful for the first time in months. Each time I experienced discomfort in my stomach, I would whisper to myself, "It's not such a big deal."

As is my wont, I began to practise that in all areas of life. Maybe missing the train and being late for work was not such a big deal. Maybe losing my cool with my colleague was not such a big deal. Maybe forgetting to wish my best friend on her birthday was not such a big deal. Maybe the aches and pains that confronted me were not such a big deal. Maybe, nothing was a big deal!

For the first time, I began to feel within me the capacity to accept my resistance to things going wrong. For the first time, I envisaged the possibility of remaining calm in the storm.

In NLP(*Neuro-linguistic Programming)*, they teach you to practise seeing yourself as bigger than your problems. Along the way, as my faith in myself and my capabilities increased steadfastly, the problems became smaller and I grew bigger.

A little mantra that I practised which goes, "I can do it; I can do it; I can do it" has helped me enormously to travel from my earlier state of frozen "I can't" to increasingly feeling confident that I could.

As confidence levels built up along with my capabilities, I began to step out of my comfort zone more and more readily. One big milestone was when I felt internally released to speak in front of audiences, which would earlier fill me with uneasiness. In a few months, I launched my writer's workshop and became a facilitator/trainer and teacher.

Through it, I was realising a 20-year-old dream. When the workshops became successful, my confidence levels rose hugely.

Another milestone moment in reducing problems to manageable proportions was when I was given a fabulous farewell gift by the publisher of *Life Positive*, Aditya Ahluwalia, in 2017. The gift was a return ticket to the US, Canada and London. I had travelled abroad only twice before, and never alone. Now, at the age of 60, contending with a few ailments to boot, I found myself contemplating travelling across two continents, four countries and seven cities all on my own.

The situation hurtled me out of my comfort zone and I was badly rattled. Nevertheless, I went ahead and did it. The more I travelled, the more confident I became. By the time I returned, I had overcome several phantom fears. The fear of using airline washrooms, the fear of handling new technology, the fear of not fitting into a White society, all disappeared into smoke. I knew that if ever I had to travel abroad alone again, I would be able to do it because I had done it once. It could be done.

Today, I have to say that I have never been more confident or felt more capable of handling situations. No, I still have not attained Nirvana, but life is infinitely more manageable.

The ultimate truth of life is that there is nothing bigger than the human spirit, for that is the emanation of the divine spark in man. We are not the puny beings we fear we are. We are mighty indeed.

Lesson #8

Only Resistance Separates Us from Bliss

I was born kicking and screaming into this world. Indeed, at a deep core meditation, I viscerally experienced my inward scream and desperate instinct to return to the womb when I discerned my parents' disappointment with my gender. The reaction was natural enough when you consider that I was the sixth daughter born to parents striving for a boy.

And since then, for the greatest part, life has dragged me kicking and screaming through its every moment. I am convinced that I never assented to being alive. That life was a project I did not want to participate in. I was always going inward and backward, while life was pushing me outward and forward. No wonder then that life and I were forever at odds. Nothing came easily to me, for I was always resisting the flow of life. Even as simple a thing as cutting a vegetable was hard for me because my resistance prevented me from being able to exert the strength needed to cut it smoothly. The same applied to writing an article or paying my bills. I resisted each chore for as long as I could, and then with every particle of my body rebelling against the action and longing to return to stasis, I reluctantly performed it. No wonder I was an underperformer. No wonder I had so little faith in myself.

My first experience of another-way-to-be arose out of my participation in a personal growth workshop, a communication workshop run by the Forum group (now Landmark Forum). We participated in some exercises where we had to talk to our parents via a partner, express what we felt, forgive and be forgiven. At the end of the two days, I felt as if I had been washed clean – that the debris inside me had miraculously disappeared, leaving me peaceful and at rest. For the first time, my attention was available in the moment. I could actually focus on seeing what was in front of my eyes instead of always seeing through a haze of thoughts and feelings.

How wondrous it felt.

Of course, that was an all-too temporary phase. But my spiritual awakening did in time offer me the keys to free myself of resistance. Awareness of what I was going through, acceptance of all that awareness revealed, and constant affirmation that I was whole, perfect and complete have gradually enabled me to draw closer and closer on the same side of life. And the more I did that, the more silky smooth existence became.

Everything became so much more manageable now that I was not being so angry, resentful or fearful of whatever was on my plate. And, of course, my confidence, peace of mind, happiness and capability increased proportionately. It became increasingly clear that all that stood between me and my whole and perfect self was my baggage of resistance.

Over the years my fears, my resistance to my fears, my resistance to my resistance and so on ad infinitum, have coated me in a thick and impenetrable armour that has taken the longest time to dissolve. The worst part about it is that it is so hard to recognise that it is the resistance that muffles up thoughts and feelings and makes the inner space seem so numb and inaccessible.

But as I continued in faith to chant that I was whole and perfect, and to retain my awareness of my thoughts and feelings for increasingly longer intervals, the resistance has begun to thaw. With that, my true self is peeping out.

While I surely have a long way to go before the resistance dissolves fully, I am beginning to realise that our thoughts and feelings are never an issue. It is our rejection of them that keeps them interred in stone.

I have found that getting angry or resenting it when someone pushes your boundaries by being overly friendly or overly bossy, is not the problem. The problem arises when we start feeling bad about our anger and perhaps our giving expression to it, then feeling bad about feeling bad, until we are so loaded with our reservoir of negativity that we simply choose to blank out.

When a passing vehicle with a loudspeaker shatters the morning tranquillity with a cacophony of noise, it is not our irritation that troubles us, but our inability to let the irritation drain away, and our tendency to justify our anger or berate ourselves for our anger that converts a simple event into something capable of toppling our mood.

When a much sought-after promotion slips out of your hands and is given to someone else, it is not your hurt, disappointment and envy of the person who gets it that is the issue. It is your inability to accept these feelings; it is your tendency to beat yourself up for having these feelings, as if the whole world were saints and only you have sinned.

Traffic jams, delays in a bus, train or plane, a curt boss, an aloof or dominating spouse, even major catastrophes: none of them would be an issue if only we could accept them instead of resisting them.

So how can we get to this space? This is, in fact, our natural space because we are not the ego. So, we don't have to do anything to get there except to dismantle the ego – that noisy, emotional, pain-making entity that we have always mistaken for ourselves.

The work lies in freeing, releasing and disidentifying from our resistance to the mind stuff. It calls for us to let go of our resistance to our anger, fear, expectations, desires and so much else. Increasingly, I am finding that when you free yourself of the resistance, the feelings and thoughts do not trouble you anymore. You are actually freed to do something about the situation instead of being in its thrall. There are many processes that have helped me on this journey. The one dominant perspective which has been my guiding light ever since I moved onto the path is my understanding that true happiness is the consequence of focussing on the happiness of others, which means that my attention needs to be on the welfare of others and not on me. The mantra that has always accompanied me these last 29 years is, "My focus is on other people's happiness, my own growth and the moment."

Along the way, many perspectives arose that enabled me to see the truth of the other more deeply and more compassionately. For one thing, I recognised by noticing it within myself, that all of us were being the very best that we could at that moment, given our backgrounds and conditioning. If we could be better, we would. I could see that the urge to be good was a deep human need, and that what caused us to veer away from that path and move into self-destructive behaviour was our own poignant disappointment with our inability to live up to our values.

I also could see that each of us had our own story that made us behave the way we did, but that our behaviour was not a reflection of our worth as human beings. Indeed, I was clear that at our core we were all whole and perfect. Knowing the story often releases our judgements. For instance, I recently met someone who struck me as a bit of a brat. Later, I learnt that both his parents were deaf and dumb. My irritation with the man was washed clean in the flood of sympathy that engulfed me.

My journey has included dropping expectations over and over again, each time at a deeper level, though I still have to let go of them completely. It has included self-acceptance and self-forgiveness, also at different levels. It has included being in the moment, each time at a deeper level. It has required me to expand my self-control, my self-respect and levels of confidence. In order to release the ego, the most important part of the work is to heal it. Only a healthy ego is capable of dropping like a ripe fruit, enabling us to naturally merge with the rest of existence.

Along the way, there came moments when I could experience a full and limpid acceptance of the moment or of a person. There were also moments when I experienced being received openly and completely. These were the markers on my path which not only told me that I was progressing but also reinforced for me the rewards of the state.

Not being in resistance is like floating on a sea of bliss, even when a storm is wildly tossing you about, shredding every aspect of your earlier life. You could be going through a divorce, a life-threatening disease, the loss of a child or reputation. And yet, you could still be cradled in radiant peace, still be fully in the moment, still deeply experience every nuance of your pain without being splintered by it.

I recall during the one year when I had the priceless privilege of being in an enlightened state, that my erstwhile boyfriend flew into a violent rage and heaped me with abuses. I responded with sprightly gaiety, "How bracing to hear this on a Monday morning!"

Freedom from resistance enables you to be available fully to the other. To see things from their perspective, to be empathetic to their story, to bat for their welfare.

It also enables you to be at peace with your situation, to forgive yourself for your part in it and to forgive others for their part.

Have I freed myself fully of resistance? No. I have to admit I am still a work in progress. But all I can say is that my level of happiness and internal freedom are directly proportional to the resistance that has left me. And when the last vestiges of resistance leave me, I will merge effortlessly into the bliss that is who I truly am.

Lesson #9

Family Matters

I have been and will always be a family person. Even though I chose not to marry, family ties matter deeply to me.

In the lonely journey of life, what a sanctuary the family is. How would a little baby ever grow into an adult without the scaffolding provided by the family? For many of us, the early childhood years of being loved, nurtured and nourished, the network of bonds we build with grandparents, parents, siblings, cousins, uncles and aunts is the cornucopia that sustains us through our lives.

Here in India, we may not have a government support system that looks after us during indigence and old age, but we have something infinitely more precious: a family that will always ensure that we do not slip through the cracks. It will help us weather sickness, financial crises, relationship crises and old age. I can never forget watching an episode of the *Oprah Winfrey Show* where a woman, a secretary, was driven to living on the streets with her daughter because a sudden illness ate so deeply into her savings that she did not have enough for rent.

Correct me if I am wrong, but I do not see too many secretaries in India living on the streets. Yes, we have millions of people living on the streets, and I am not insensitive to their plight, but I do maintain that the family network shields the great majority from sharing that fate. I don't deny that many families do not offer this support and there are millions who may be foundering in the storms of life alone and uncared for. But, by and large, most of us can count on our families in a way that we generally cannot on our friends or other relationships.

I was lucky to have been born into a large family, an almost extinct entity in today's times. We are six sisters and I am the youngest of this brood. By the great grace of God, we are all still alive, though I, the youngest, turned 63 in June 2020. We provide a vital support system to each other. We always did that. For instance, soon after college, I teamed up with my fourth sister, Susan, to live in rented apartments or as paying guests until she bought her own house, in which I lived for close to eight years until I became editor of *Society* and was given a company flat. When my second sister, Molly, had to undergo a uterus operation, my third sister, Leela, hurried down from Delhi, leaving behind her husband and young daughters in order to nurse her. When my father developed a brain tumour, the entire family descended upon Vizag, coming from Kerala, Mumbai and Kolkata. Until my father passed away, one or the other of my sisters was always there to help my mother look after him. This is what families do.

Happily, our kinship has only deepened with age and with the passing of our parents. Susan and I never married. Today, my sisters Leela and Molly are widowed. Leela lives alone in Cochin, while my sister Molly lives in Mumbai, where Susan, Sheela, my fifth sister, and I reside. My eldest sister, Mariamma, lives in a small Kerala town called Kozhencherry. Except for Molly's children, Naveen and Nisha, and Mariamma's younger son, most of my nieces and nephews are living out of India or staying away from their parents. Naturally, the sisters gravitated closer to each other. We have helped each other weather a host of ailments which includes cancer. We have banded together to care for our mother during a lengthy period of paralysis for the last two and a half years of her life.

I always thought I would leave Mumbai after retirement and settle in some beautiful verdant spot. But I now recognise that I need my family, and that my family needs me.

Our deepest and most sacred ties are with the family, whether natal or those created through marriage. Our most intimate moments, our deepest joys and deepest sorrows stem from the family. The family is also our most immediate and perhaps most important tool for growth. Through lifetimes of give and take, we have forged individual relationships with each member of the family. With some, we enjoy a deep sense of love; with others, despite knowing them for a lifetime, we experience insurmountable barriers. With still others, we are locked in dispute, conflict and violent hatred. What a palette of possibilities. And how important for us to heal these primary relationships in order to free ourselves from the grip of our karmic bondage with each other. Even if we do not know this, and even if we duck resolving our disputes with family members, the family still usually remains our primary and most important source of sustenance.

This means we also need to give it that importance in our lives. All too often, especially during our childhood and youth, we tend to take the family for granted, especially all that our parents do for us, and prioritise our friends and peers. This is perhaps a natural process to help the budding adult forge an independent life, but all too often we thoughtlessly end up diminishing family bonds. I remember that when my mother and I were living together, there was a phase when I was enmeshed in a relationship. Every night after coming home from work and having a hurried dinner, I would take the phone in my hand and get into a lengthy conversation with my friend, uncomfortably aware that in our little cosy family of two, I was dragging in a new entity. In doing so, I was making our relationship less.

I also could see that there are certain roles that belong to the family which cannot be trespassed upon. For one thing, they are the principal caregivers, and if we allow friends to play that role, despite the availability of family, we are sending a lethal message to them on their importance in our lives.

Family comes first. If a family dinner clashes with an evening with the boys or with the girls, go with the family. If you are in the midst of a conversation with a family member and a friend calls, complete your conversation with them before calling back your friend.

And when it comes to raising a family of your own, you can never forget that the welfare of your children is paramount and must supersede all your concerns. In the hurly-burly of creating a successful career track, many parents, particularly men, tend to neglect the family. This is also one of the most common regrets they have when they grow older. Relationships, particularly relationships with the family, are vital for our spiritual and emotional well-being. We need to spend time and effort in nurturing, nourishing and healing these equations. In the book, *The 7 Habits of Highly Effective Families*, Stephen Covey, another passionate advocate of family values, advocates setting aside family time every week, spending one-on-one time with each member of the family and going on family holidays. A friend of mine lives with her two sons and when the elder got married, she spent a great deal of time even before he brought the bride home, in creating the ideal bond she would like to share with her daughter-in-law. For all of them, Sunday is family time, and no one is allowed to trespass on that.

Parents know that sacrifice is the foundation on which a family is built. Constant and consistent prioritising of their children's happiness, health and welfare keeps the family together. For further growth of the family even when its members are adults and living apart, it is only the commitment of each person to be available when needed, to stay in touch on a regular basis and to constantly affirm to themselves and to others their importance in our lives that will keep us together.

Lesson #10

You Can't Go It Alone

In our adolescence and early 20s, nothing is more attractive than the idea of cutting off all messy human ties and living alone. "I am a rock. I am an island," sing Simon and Garfunkle, ending, "and a rock feels no pain. And an island never cries."

Technology in all its manifestations powerfully reinforces the illusion of self-sufficiency. There was once a time when phones in India were rare commodities, and we had to perforce depend on cooperative neighbours to make urgent phone calls.

In its early years, TV brought together the neighbourhood as we all huddled together in one house to watch *Hum Log*, *Buniyaad* or *Mahabharata*; and the VCR enabled us to spend Saturday nights *en famille* watching blockbuster Hollywood or Bollywood treats.

Today, technology alienates, divides and thrusts us even further into our aloneness. A phone in hand and earplugs firmly in one's ears, we can walk the streets plugged into our own private world. Social media with its incessant updates and pings gives us the illusion of being connected without the risk of intimacy. Most of us have an array of devices that effectively enable us to get by without interacting too much with neighbours or the world at large.

Fortunately, *satyamev jayate* (only the truth prevails). And so it is that as we move into our 20s and 30s or even as late as our 40s, we realise that we just cannot do without people. Beyond our tight little nuclear world lies a whole web of ties that we desperately need. We need friends. We need family. We need community. There is a limit beyond which we cannot do it alone. A crisis is what usually brings about this realisation. Your spouse falls dangerously ill. Who will look after your kids? Who will relieve you from hospital duty? Who will feed you?

The very people who we once ignored or considered dispensable – family, friends and neighbours – will usually surge out in support.

I myself came face to face with the need for the other during my father's brain haemorrhage in 1984. Except for Molly, who then lived in Vizag close to my parents, the rest of us sisters were scattered in Kerala, Mumbai and Kolkata.

By the time we reached Vizag, the Church community of which my parents were active members, had taken over. My father had been admitted to hospital and was lovingly being cared for by a doctor who belonged to our community. A stream of Church members flowed into the hospital with food and offers of hospital duty.

I, who was an alienated atheist at that point of time, was moved to the depths of my soul by the kinship that I witnessed during the weeks my father was in the hospital. I recognised that apart from its religious function, the church plays a vital social role, which enables everyone to plug into an identity larger than their own, and to nourish and be nourished by it.

The same lesson was reinforced during the period when my mother was paralysed. There were times when I desperately needed a helping hand. When I tentatively reached out to a neighbour, she joyously came home, and together we looked after my mother. I realised then that help is all around us, if we would but ask. Many people hold back from offering help unasked for fear of intruding. But their hearts ache for you, and they are all too willing to support you the moment you ask them.

Crises apart, we learn at some point or other how much we need people. We are social beings and, in order to be happy and healthy, we need to be plugged into a network of relationships. There is enormous research to support this stand. Recently, several reports have pointed out that the two significant factors that increase longevity are the number of casual conversations you have with people around you such as neighbours, watchmen or vegetable vendors, and the number of deep relationships you have with people, the marker for which would be their willingness to come to your help even at 4 a.m.

There is a deep hunger in us that only gets satiated through meaningful human contact. Most couples stay together in stale marriages simply because of that human contact – someone to cook for, someone to watch the news with, someone to crib about the Government to.

Without adequate human contact, we will fade away and die. In his book, *Love and Survival*, Dr Dean Ornish, the American doctor who famously bypassed the bypass through holistic measures such as group therapy, a healthy diet and meditation, writes about a horrible experiment conducted by a 13th-century German king called Frederick ll. The king decided to take a few babies away from their mothers at birth and raise them in the best of conditions – the best food, clothing, shelter and medical care. The only caveat was that the babies would never be spoken to, picked up or touched by human hands. Each one of these babies died. Human touch was much more important to them than any material comfort.

This is a truth that becomes more and more imperative as we move towards the age of Artificial Intelligence. How tempting for many of us to cut off needy and conflict-ridden human relationships for dulcet robots who will obey our every order.

But this is just what we need to resist. No matter how difficult, no matter how frustrating, we need our fellow human beings. It is through them that we learn our biggest lessons and experience our greatest joys. What J. Krishnamurti, the maverick philosopher, observed is fundamental: "To be is to be related." We are enmeshed in a network of relationships – with our books, toys, pets and all the human beings we encounter. We cannot duck this, even if we want to. To live in harmony with our fellow human beings is one of our biggest tasks. Unless we can do it, the great glory of human existence – the achievement of enlightenment – will be denied to us.

The West is particularly prone to the illusion of self-sufficiency. Children leave the parental home at 18 and take up their own apartment. Since the cost of human labour is prohibitive, they learn to do everything by themselves, armed with a plethora of gadgets. Where most of us in India can afford the services of a maid, only the super-rich can do so there. Nor can you avail of the services of a *dhobhi*, a CA, a computer maintenance guy, someone to repair your mobile for you, and a host of other services that we don't think twice about availing.

Most of all, the dearth of human contact is resulting in a glut of mental, emotional and spiritual problems that are steeping people in suffering. We, in India, are rapidly going in the same direction, unless we can wake up and take corrective steps.

A friend shared that her son and daughter-in-law rarely contact her, and discourage her from contacting them, too. They took no step towards inviting her over to Singapore where they live, until my friend self-invited herself so she could finally see her grandson. My friend is one of the finest persons I know. So, personal enmity is out of the question. More likely, the couple assumes that they are sufficient unto themselves and do not need anyone else. My mother used to say that we even need the crow flying overhead. Indeed, we do. Oneness is our ultimate reality and it is pointless to imagine that we can get by on our own.

So, get out of your cloak of self-sufficiency and reach out to another. Your contact may nourish them, and it will surely nourish you.

Lesson #11

Nature Has the Answers

Even though we often rue that we have taken birth on Planet Earth without learning what life is and how we are meant to live it, the Creator has scattered innumerable clues for us in Nature. If we would but embrace Nature as our guru, as sage Dattatreya did (one of the premier members of the Nath Sampradaya, and a very significant figure in Hinduism), we, too, would get enlightened. Lord Dattatreya attributed his enlightenment to 24 gurus, which included the earth, the five elements, the sky, sun and moon, the elephant, python, honeybee, deer and fish. From the earth, he learnt the qualities of forgiveness, unselfishness and the capacity to bear burdens. The vast firmament of the sky taught him expansiveness and limitlessness, while the air's all-pervading nature, unaffected by anything, reminded him of consciousness.

There is no better education than the teaching Nature provides. If we were to spend a few months in Nature, we would emerge with deeper insights and more intuitive wisdom than we would after four years in a college.

Nature is harmony manifest. When a new leaf unfurls on a stem, it will do it in a way that does not obstruct the other leaves from getting sunlight. When a bud blossoms among a cluster, it, too, will seek to fit into a gap instead of pushing another out of the way. All the cycles of Nature, such as the arising of darkness and dawn, the moon's waxing and waning, the change of seasons, the blooming of a flower or the ripening of a fruit happen in an orderly, unhurried manner. The deep intelligence so evident in all of Nature is sufficient proof for those who look that there has to be a Creator, sustaining and maintaining the Universe. The Invisible God is visible in every atom of Her Creation.

Nature is love personified. All religions proclaim that God is love and that it is love that moves the Universe. We see this sublime love in the working of every aspect of Nature. What is it that causes the air to condense, form clouds and finally precipitate into rain that falls upon the parched earth and helps her produce food for her children? Love. What causes the tree to labour silently but constantly, to produce fruits it will never consume, or the plant to grow flowers it does not need? Surely, love? What causes water to sacrifice itself by moistening the earth? What causes birds to greet every dawn, no matter how wretched the weather, but love? Love causes dry leaves to flutter to the ground without a worry. Love vibrates through every aspect of creation, and if we were but more conscious, we would be aware of it.

Nature is stillness personified. Nature is forever doing. Fresh flowers and leaves are growing, old leaves are falling, fresh roots are snaking through the soil, crops are ripening, yet all this vigorous activity is executed in utter silence. The tranquil expanse of a field of emerald paddy bears no evidence to the constant growth in action. Unlike the stress and strain we put on ourselves, Nature wields her miracles in surrender. Action happens, she does nothing. No wonder being in Nature is so tranquillising. It connects us to the silence within us.

Above all, Nature has no ego. Unlike our selfish, self-centred and desire-driven agendas, Nature wants nothing for herself. She lives to serve the larger whole. Is there anything more humble or resilient than the grass, allowing all to trample upon it, and yet willing itself to rise again? The earth itself bears every degradation we have heaped on her, and silently continues to supply us with food and water.

There is no bigger giver than Nature, for it sustains all life on earth. Even its most intransigent moods, such as mighty earthquakes, tsunamis, typhoons, floods or forest fires, are all part of its intricate balancing act so it can continue to sustain life. What a magnificent force Nature is. How high, lofty and noble. What could be a better role model?

It all boils down to this: Nature is the embodiment of the enlightened state, for it is synonymous with love, order, harmony, stillness and generosity. The more we surround ourselves with Nature, the more we will awaken to *our* true nature. This is why our Indian *rishis* and sages were forest dwellers, for Nature was both master and monastery.

But even in more mundane matters, Nature is the ultimate muse. So many of the asanas in yoga have been derived by the movements of animals and Nature. Take the *vrikshasana* (tree pose), *parvatasana* (mountain asana), the downward-facing dog, cat pose, fish pose and cow face pose.

The cure for countless ailments came to inspired *vaidyas* (Ayurvedic healers) who were guided to specific herbs and plants in Nature. It is my certain assertion that Nature holds the solution for every ailment, if only we were still and surrendered enough to intuit it.

For artists and designers, poets and writers, Nature is the ultimate inspiration. The beauty so manifest in Nature is in itself one of God's biggest gifts. Its colours, shapes, forms and patterns have sustained all manner of artists and craftsmen since mankind first began to make cave paintings.

For the humanitarian, Nature is a powerful lesson in diversity. A rose is different from a dahlia, which is different from a tuberose. Yet they can offset and support each other in a bouquet. The leaves of a bamboo tree are different from the leaves of a banana tree or a coconut tree. And yet all three can live in the same environment and add beauty to it. How much they have to teach us human beings who are forever discriminating against each other on the basis of colour, caste, community or creed. How much we have diminished our heritage and our culture by razing and destroying all that does not match with our ideas or is different from us.

For packaging experts, what better inspiration than Nature? From the fragility of the egg to the carcass of the coconut shell or the peanut shell, nature's packaging is always ingenious and appropriate, not to mention 100 per cent biodegradable.

Above all, let us remember that we are a part of this very Nature, not apart from it. Our attempts to control and dominate it, to raze it down and build roads, buildings and factories instead, our polluting of air, water and earth will all ricochet on us. It is already happening. Hopefully, it will be the scorpion sting that will awaken us from our stupor and compel us to take the steps that will save our beloved Mother Earth and ourselves, too.

Lesson #12

Do the Work You Were Born For

"Blessed is he who has found his work. Let him ask no other blessedness."

— Thomas Carlyle

As one who was fortunate enough to have found her work, I heartily agree. I was not born with a treasure trove of talents. In fact, I had only one in modest measure, which was an ability to write. An avid reader, writing followed naturally; and eventually journalism emerged as a career option.

And though in the early years, I did not exactly cover myself with glory, my job as a feature writer in magazines was interesting, occasionally stimulating and never routine. I consider myself a student of human nature, so meeting and writing about people was fascinating. Yet, I was a drifter; I never really attempted to excel in my profession until my awakening cleared out all the shadows in my mind and filled me with the zeal to live.

By then I had been the editor of *Society* for a year. I continued for a few more years, spending that time honing my skills as a writer and editor, and learning to handle people. But it was only after I truly discerned my mission, which was to create awareness of a holistic way of life, which in turn would lead to a Spiritual Age, that I really felt I had found my life's work.

I remember how immensely blessed I felt when I joined *Life Positive* magazine and began to focus exclusively on writing about body, mind and spirit. Almost everyone I met became a friend. The articles I wrote not just supported my own spiritual journey, but also that of thousands of readers. How often I was lucky enough to have readers tell me that what I had written had changed their lives.

After I left *Society* to join *Life Positive*, I took a decision that I would never write about anything except spirituality, and even though I went through rather a difficult financial period, I stood by it. I always felt one with the magazine. I could discern no difference between me and the magazine. My perspectives and my priorities were exactly reflected in the magazine as well. Later, when I became its editor, this kind of affinity became a real gift because I never had to think about what fitted in *Life Positive* and what did not. Thus, it was possible to ensure a consistency in the magazine's identity. This sort of twin-ness is the rarest of rare blessings for an editor and, when one has it, one really has no business pining for anything else. I remember many years ago, a business editor editor briefly became the editor of a male adult magazine called *Debonair*, and to suit his comfort zone, the editor began to shift the action from the bedroom to the boardroom. Sounds ludicrous, but it is true.

My own experience has led me to firmly believe that as far as possible, one should do work one is fitted for, and that is an authentic form of self-expression. Sometimes, that is too precious a luxury if you have a family to feed and bills to pay. But whenever possible, please, please, let go of that plush lifestyle before you become addicted to it, and go out on a limb. Become a healer or a writer. A chef or an oracle. A sportsperson or a historian. A blogger or a farmer.

Each of us has so much to offer to the world. One of the prime reasons we have taken incarnation in these times is to offer our uniqueness to the world. Let us not compromise the joy and dignity of doing the right work simply out of love for a posh lifestyle.

If there is one thing I am sure of, it is this. Comfort is never the thing to go after. The moment we get entrapped by comfort and do not want to make choices because it will mean living in Malad (a suburb in Mumbai where I happen to live) rather than Malabar Hill (the Beverly Hills equivalent of Mumbai), or taking an auto rather than driving a Merc, you have got to remember that you are putting your growth and happiness on the line. The world does not need a long dreary line of MBAs, IT professionals, engineers, bankers and doctors that colleges and universities are churning out. It needs people who love what they do, who will put their all into it and who will innovate fearlessly and joyously. It needs people who will take their profession to the cutting edge of excellence because of their passion for it.

I had a young colleague called Vikram Hazra in my last year at *Society* magazine, who was an exceptional singer and guitarist. He was an exceptional writer too, but I was delighted when the lad took the path less chosen, joined the Art of Living and moved to Bangalore to be with his guru, despite familial objection. In time, he became one of AOL's most gifted singers and now holds bhajan concerts all over the world, having earned innumerable fans. His life has opened up uniquely, and all because he had the courage to follow his heart.

Prateek Kuhad, the Delhi-based singer/songwriter whose albums have earned him international acclaim, and whose legion of fans includes Barack Obama, was all set to do the tried and tested by studying Maths and Economics from New York University, and had even got a job as a consultant in a firm when he, fortunately, threw it all up to pursue music. His debut album in 2015, *In Tokens and Charms*, earned him an MTV Europe Music Award, Indie Album of the Year honours from iTunes, Best Pop Artist at the Radio City Freedom Awards, and first place in the prestigious International Songwriting Competition. He has not looked back since.

I often wonder how many creative geniuses could be mouldering away in banks and government offices, either because they did not know what else to do, or because of parental pressure. It takes time for us to figure out what we are meant to do, or what it is that we long to do. In our early years, most of us are drawn to professions like acting, modelling or cricket because of the allure of glamour. It takes time for the scales to fall from our eyes, and to know ourselves better. At the same time, one can't blame parents, either. Having won Independence only a few decades ago, parents only had one agenda – safety and security – and this was pushed on to their progeny.

Today's times are different. Parents are more prosperous (though there is no telling what the post-Covid 19 society will bring in its wake) and children more adventurous and risk-friendly. Besides, the burgeoning social media world has brought up a multitude of opportunities and professions today, and youngsters are aware of them, too.

So, if you are hesitating between being a musician and a middle manager, you really have talent and your parents can afford to subsidise you for a while, take a chance and jump into your dream. You may fail, but at least you would have tried. And if you succeed? Well, your life will expand magically and fill you with an ineffable joy and satisfaction. You may well end up earning fame and fortune also. Above all, you will have made a contribution to humanity through harnessing your unique talents and skills.

Lesson #13

Freedom of Will Is Sacrosanct

Our crowning glory and our greatest peril is the biggest gift the Creator has given man: freedom of will.

Man has been given the freedom to craft his own way in the world, unlike other creatures of the earth, all of whom are guided by the Creator's own intelligence. Man alone is free to go wayward and wild, or be winsome and wonderful. Yes, there are consequences to every single thought, word or deed but, otherwise, the Creator has left us free. What a staggering testimony to the trust God places in us. This is how high we stand in Her esteem. This is the unconditional faith She has in our ability to get it right.

And right now, we need this assurance. Look at how we have used our free will! Look at the piteous plight our beautiful Planet Earth is in. A ravaged and destroyed environment. Polluted and despoiled air, water and soil. Thousands of species extinct, and thousands more on the brink of it. Mankind itself locked in strife and misery. Our report card makes grim reading. Should we wonder why the Coronavirus came calling, and locked the whole world indoors while Nature set about repairing some of the ravages we have brought upon it?

And yet, the wonder of it all is that God continues to give us freedom of will. She continues to allow us to think and do what we wish. Surely, God knew even before She embarked on this audacious experiment that we might destroy the planet. And yet, She did not falter. Can one even conceive of a love like this?

Sages have said that so sacrosanct is our freedom of will in God's eyes, that She does not ever enter our minds unasked. Our mind is sacred territory, and She would not dream of trespassing. She does not even ask us to love Her or believe in Her. She waits patiently for us to return to Her, as and when we choose to.

So, if God respects our freedom of will absolutely, can we not at least strive to be likewise? Can we also not show a modicum of the same forbearance towards our fellow human beings? Instead of riding roughshod over others, or bullying and browbeating them, can we step back and allow them to exercise the self-determination with which they are born?

Parents, can you recognise that your child has been born with a sovereign freedom of will? Can you refrain from curbing or controlling them and binding them to your will? Can you remember that you do not own the child, but are merely their guardian, and that your job is to raise the child into a balanced, self-aware and self-respecting human being who can use their freedom of will responsibly and for the welfare of mankind?

Husbands, can you recognise that your wives are not your property, to be used as you wish, but sovereign human beings bestowed with a will of their own that God dare not interfere with? Can you respect her and honour her need to be her own person and to determine her own life?

Can bosses recognise that their subordinates are also gifted with the same freedom of will that they have been given, and that simply because they work for them does not mean they own them?

Can our politicians recognise that we citizens have been given the same sacrosanct will that they have and treat us with the respect that we deserve?

Can religious leaders recognise that we are no less than they are in the eyes of God, and refrain from liaising between God and us?

The ego's heinous need to control and rule over others is one of the primary reasons for the misery on this planet. Man has always looked to control life by conquering the other. The other could be Nature, it could be fellow human beings or it could be countries. In the name of patriotism, religion or safety, man has waged innumerable wars, destroyed the planet and tyrannised millions.

Petty domestic tyranny continues in every part of the globe. Parents determining their child's course of study and future career, even though the child may be called to do something else. Parents deciding the child's future spouse or value system, or trampling upon their individuality in order to control them better. Husbands abusing their wives physically, sexually and psychologically. Wife-beating is still prevalent, while dowry deaths and honour killing figure in this country's own Gallery of Horrors. Women tyrannising over their husbands and children and, of course, their daughter-in-law.

Everywhere, we casually step on people's freedom of will. When we read our partner's Whatsapp chats or Facebook page without their knowledge, we are disrespecting the sanctity of their minds.

How can we become more respectful of other people's freedom of will and more vigilant about our own? Personally, I am convinced that only sound self-esteem can help us do both. As we learn to love and accept ourselves unconditionally, we will naturally learn to establish our boundaries, enhance our self-respect and release our individuality. Simultaneously, because our self-love will heal our emotional and psychological needs, we will no longer aspire to power over others and peacefully give them the space to be themselves.

In time, as we grow in self-esteem as a society, our systems, our politics and relationship with Nature will also change.

The place to begin is with ourselves, and with inner work. Let us start the process of inner spring-cleaning, healing ourselves of our wounds and building our confidence and capability. Only in that way will we finally align with the Creator's vision, of a world where no one will control nor allow themselves to be controlled.

Lesson #14

We Are Not Alone

I vividly recall how random, meaningless and impenetrable my life was before my spiritual awakening illuminated life and its mysteries to me. Nothing made sense and my life seemed to be going nowhere.

However, after my awakening, I was fascinated to find an inner coherence forming. As I became more and more adept at focussing on the happiness of the other, I could, for the first time in my life, experience strength entering my being. The practice of self-effacement, of prioritising the other's welfare required great self-control and sacrifice. Each time I managed it successfully, I felt an inner power pulsing within.

For the first time in my life, I felt as if I were growing and even moving. Where earlier my life had seemed to be static, I was now journeying purposefully. Towards what, I still did not know coherently, but certainly I was going somewhere. That sensation of movement became even more pronounced over the next few months. Suddenly, life and I seemed on the same page. Indeed, life seemed to be actively on my side. If I had a question in my head, somehow in the next few days I would find an answer, either from my inner self, from a conversation with a friend or from a newspaper article or book.

In some time, I began to recognise that I was on a journey towards growth and perfection, and that the path was being laid for me before my eyes. Wonder-struck, I would see that with each day, there were changes in me, that new questions were dawning and, in the course of time, getting answered. I could also see that with each new question and its answer, an earlier understanding of life would be resoldered and made broader and bigger. Half-truths were giving way to larger truths and helping me understand life in a deeper way.

But perhaps even more beautiful than the resolution of the mysteries was the realisation that unlike science's stipulation that the Universe was random and fragmented, it was neither. There was a power, an intelligent power that seemed to be aware of me and my quest and was wanting me to succeed in it. How stupendous! That discovery healed me of my deepest layer of loneliness. I was not alone in this human enterprise. I was supported by what seemed to be all of life. Later, as I became more aware of the spiritual movement and read hundreds of books explaining life, after-life and so on, I learnt how each of us has guardian angels assigned to us, and that we are indeed looked after by the Masters and a whole legion of souls.

Inspiration and guidance can come to us in many forms such as dreams, thoughts or counsel from others. There are even many evolved souls who take incarnation to play the role of angels in people's lives. A dear friend told me that she went through so much trauma as a child that she actually took to smoking at the age of 13 or so. Once, on a school trip abroad, she escaped from a visit to a church in order to go out and grab a smoke. A stranger saw her and told her that her life was too precious and she was too young to be smoking, and that she had better pull herself together. That counsel from a total stranger changed her life and she began to take steps to come out of the black hole she had slipped into. Today, she is a highly successful and much-loved businesswoman. Surely, that stranger was nothing less than an angel?

Even those of our loved ones who leave us for the other side always watch out for us. We may not be able to see or hear them, but they can see and hear us. A friend of mine has just moved into a lovely plush three-bedroom apartment after looking at 27 flats. She would have given up the search at the 27th out of sheer exhaustion, but the agent told her that there was one more flat which they had not shown her simply because the owner was fastidious about the tenant. On her way to see the house, she spoke to her late father in her mind. She reminded him of how protective he had been of her and her sisters. And now, here she was going into strange people's houses in the company of unknown real estate agents. Could he not end the search for her? Soon, they reached the flat. To her delight, it was beautiful and she fell in love with it at first sight. But would the owner relent? To her surprise, the owner recognised her. It turned out that he was a close friend of her father's, and had promised her father to always be there for her, since she had chosen to stay unmarried. Unfortunately, he and his family had emigrated to the US soon after, which is why he was here to rent out his apartment. Long story short, the apartment was hers, and the landlord even gave her an exhaustive list of vendors she would need, along with their numbers. He even introduced her to some 10 neighbours in the building so she would not be alone. Surely, it was no coincidence that she had petitioned her father just before seeing the house?

So, let us never feel isolated or alone. We are deeply loved and taken care of. Always. Yes, our karma may determine untoward events and circumstances, but even so, there are far fewer accidents than there could be. In his book, *The Road Less Travelled*, the psychologist, Scott L. Peck writes about how, as a child, he had slipped under a speeding car one snowy day. The car went over him without harming him, leaving him wonderstruck at the way we are looked after. The late Dada Vaswani, head of the Pune-based Sadhu

Vaswani Mission, once observed that a merciful Providence truncates all except the unavoidable consequences of our karma. God's grace and love watch over every moment of our lives.

Lesson #15

Free Will and Destiny Are Intertwined

All of us have pitted our heads against the subtle relationship between free will and destiny. Can we determine every twist and turn of our lives, or is destiny the determining factor? Those who are dynamic and wield their wills powerfully in order to get what they want, will root for free will. Those who are unable to move their lives in the direction of their dreams and have felt themselves clamped by the iron hand of unsupportive circumstances, will vote for destiny.

But the equation is not quite as simple as that. The relationship between free will and destiny keeps changing and evolving as we change and evolve. So the same person may have different views on the subject as their experiences and insights shift and change.

Take me, for instance. Having been an extremely passive and lazy person for the early part of my life, I never felt I had the power to challenge extenuating circumstances and move triumphantly in the direction I wanted to. Every block and hurdle seemed like a mountain to me. Thus, until I was 33, my life was remarkably stationary, unless the Universe pushed me here and there. I had no romantic relationships, I chose safe jobs and hunkered into them until circumstances forced me to leave them, I developed no interests or hobbies,

I took no calculated risks and so on. I was in survival mode and destiny was my boss.

My awakening changed all that dramatically. It was as if a fuse inside me had been repaired and I was effulgent with hope and dreams. Now that I knew how to live, I couldn't wait to get started. At this point, my understanding of destiny and free will changed dramatically, too. I could see that there was a dynamic interplay between the two. Stuff happens – illnesses, relationship challenges, financial meltdowns and politics at work. These situations can be seen as destiny throwing the dice. How you play the game can be seen as your free will at work. If you react, withdraw, complain, cry or draw negative conclusions about yourself or life, then destiny wins this round. If however, you circle back, learn your lessons, see where you went wrong and take steps to resolve the problem, then you have used your free will to collaborate with destiny to move forward in your life.

As all the motivational speakers tell us, life may hand us a lemon, but free will can help us make lemonade out of it. Thus, simply by making the most of whatever destiny throws us, we can retain free will and grow prodigiously in capability and responsibility.

Since our free will has to be strong and powerful to get us out of limiting circumstances, it follows that we will easily exert our will to create the life we want. We move house, city or country. We change our jobs or even our professions. We learn art, theatre, salsa, calligraphy and baking. We become entrepreneurs and start our own business. We leave dead marriages and renew our lives. We take courses and attend workshops. We become healers and therapists, writers and artists. We return to life all that we have received from it.

Life opens up and expands as we begin to increasingly feel that nothing is beyond us. Destiny now appears to be a benign teacher who throws us these gauntlets only so that we can grow and expand even more. Destiny and free will work in tandem to ongoingly increase and expand our potential and life.

But that does not tell the whole story. It may happen that try as we might, some things may not land up on our plate. For some reason, money seems to elude you. Or marriage may never knock on your door. Or that illness that you have contended with all your life simply will not go away. That is when you face the intransigent face of destiny, whose other name is karma. Some things are simply not meant for us in this lifetime and we will have to come to terms with that.

And as time moves on, there comes a point when self-centred desires seem to dissipate. We no longer pine to see foreign lands or possess that diamond set. Going to the mall no longer excites us, nor are we consumed with the desire to sample new and different foods. For that matter, even sex no longer compels. Free of the imp of desire, we become more spacious and peaceful. Instead of trotting around restlessly, we seem to be dropping an anchor.

And as you look back on the long arm of your life, you begin to see with increasing clarity that every last situation and circumstance has been knitted skillfully by an unknown hand to make you who you are, and to bring you to where you have got. Even the dead-end job that you hated showed you where your calling was; the failed marriage taught you vital lessons about relationships that have enriched your equations with friends and family; the allergy that stopped you from eating wheat or milk products has kept you slim, fit and healthy.

In everything, a higher intelligence seems to have integrated your life. It hits you like a thunderbolt that there really is no such thing as free will. Every thought and every deed, every idea and every project has been a happening. Nothing has been created by us. It is God and only God who runs our life. It has always only been destiny.

But this new discovery is a polar opposite from the earlier one of destiny as a straitjacket that imprisons us. Instead, we do what we are called upon to do. We gracefully co-create with the power running our lives by doing what we are meant to do rather than what we want to do. Our goals and plans now are focussed on the larger good, instead of our own, and everything happens peacefully and easily. We seem to have found the levers to life and so we float along, ceaselessly but peacefully doing.

Lesson #16

Pursue Life

"I went to the woods because I wished to live deliberately, to front only the essential facts of life, and see if I could not learn what it had to teach, and not, when I came to die, discover that I had not lived. I did not wish to live what was not life, living is so dear; nor did I wish to practice resignation, unless it was quite necessary."

— Henry David Thoreau

In this short paragraph, Thoreau has masterfully put forward a case for life. We are here to live, to experience, to fully realise the glory of existence. Instead, our present-day lifestyle, which is a pursuit of comfort, convenience and luxury, pits us against life. We swaddle ourselves so much that life becomes muffled and distanced. Instead of walking and being fully available to the elements and to Nature, we *exercycle* in the sterile environs of home. Instead of taking public transport and being in the bracing presence of our fellow human beings, we bowl along in isolation in our chauffeur-driven cars. Instead of picnicking on the beach or in the woods, we spend the day in the mall. And when we tire of all the tame living, we go to Esselworld or some other amusement park in order to get some kicks. We holiday in fancy resorts in fancy places and spend our time sitting by the swimming pool sipping drinks or, even worse, watching TV in our hotel room while all of life waits for us to embrace it.

'Civilisation' can often refine to the point of straining life out. Life waits for us in the fragrance of a basket of jasmine carried by a woman vendor. It looks through the eyes of an adorable street puppy. It softly caresses us when we walk on springy grass. It soothes us as we sit under the shelter of a tree. It thrills us through a thunderstorm. It teaches us through the wisdom of the elderly. It entrances us through the smile of the newborn. It entices us into jungles and mountains. It leads us into country roads thick with flowering vines and old trees. It embraces us during intimate moments of communion with family and friends. It thrives when we sing, dance, paint, write or act.

Sadly, we are increasingly withdrawing from it into the barren embrace of social media and technology. Instead of facing life head-on through meeting or even chatting, we play safe with messages that may give the illusion of intimacy but do not offer any.

Even as I write this, I am in the middle of a writer's retreat that I organised for some of my close comrades. Some of our friends are leaving early, so this morning, we decided to have a closure ceremony for them. They shared so movingly some of the deep insights into themselves that they received inadvertently that some of the members burst into tears because they threw their own shadows so sharply into the light. We wept, we hugged, we kissed, we shared and, at the end of it, the group emerged feeling cleansed and perhaps, in small ways, healed. This was life at its resonant best, and no amount of FB or Whatsapp sharing could possibly have compared. We are going back richer, wholer and with a deep appreciation and love for each other.

Daisaku Ikeda, the Japanese spiritual head of the Soka Gakkai movement, reflects movingly in his book, *Hope is a Decision*:

> "Science and technology have given humanity undreamt of power, bringing invaluable benefits to our lives. But this has been accompanied by the tendency to distance ourselves from life, to objectify and reduce everything around us to numbers and things."

What is the cost of our shying away from life so markedly? We become increasingly less alive, less happy, less vibrant, less dynamic, less powerful and less involved. Our life force dwindles to the extent that we reject life. Is it any wonder that depression has ensnared so many of our young and vulnerable?

Deprived of the vitality, of the life sap that is the essence of our being, we become enmeshed in possessions, in emotional and psychological needs, in all sorts of addictions and obsessions. The robust mental and physical health that should be ours by right, had we reached out to life, eludes us, and we begin to decline physically, mentally, emotionally and spiritually.

I remember reading the ecstatic account of a tribal man who was so in love with life, with the streams and trees, animals and birds of his habitat that he passionately expressed his hope to return to life over and over again.

Life nourishes us. We flourish in its embrace. The more we free ourselves of the suffocating veils of comfort and step out into life unfettered and free, the more vibrant and joyous our lives will be. Go out to the bazaars and spend some time in the thick of the mill. It may be hot and uncomfortable, but the buzz of the people around, the vendors selling their wares at the top of their voices, loaders carrying vast baskets on their heads, passengers milling around excitedly looking, feeling, smelling and tasting the myriad products on display, will fill you with vitality. Make sure to strike up conversations with a stranger or two. I know of nothing more delightful than to discover the friend hidden within the stranger. Allow life to lead you into adventures and journeys not of your own choosing. A friend wants you to go paragliding. Despite your reservations you go, and you encounter a wild part of you that you never knew existed. Or a young girl faints in the local train and in the process of taking her home to her family, you once again meet life in the new parts of the town you get to see. Consider boarding a local train, getting off at a station outside city limits and spending a few beautiful hours wandering in the countryside. Spending time with old people, babies and children, innocent villagers, with nature, and with animals, increases our stores of resilience and vitality. Our immunity levels surge up and our health improves substantially. If we want to live we need to immerse ourselves in life. Any other way spells death.

Lesson #17

Meditate on Happiness

A wit once said that life was a riddle wrapped in a mystery inside an enigma.

How hard it is to understand life. How confusing are its effects. Nothing follows the rules of logic. You may deserve to come first in class but you plunge into the middle ranks while someone not half as smart makes the cut. You may have it dinned into your head that you have to be good, but all around you people are manipulative, dishonest and opportunistic. Moreover, your goodness has often been mistaken for naiveté, and people have taken advantage of you. So why should you be good? And even worse, how do you reconcile with the complete uncertainty of life? In a heartbeat, you can have an accident, fall in love, win a lottery or die of a heart attack. In short, life appears unfair, unreasonable and uncertain, an impenetrable conundrum that has us by the tail.

Nevertheless, the central driver in all our lives is to try and understand this thing called life and how to live it. Of course, many of us do not get there because we are too preoccupied with simply surviving. Life can be a brutal tyrant pushing us relentlessly to put food on the table and clothes on our children's backs. But for many of us, the question never lets up. How are we supposed to live?

Fortunately for all of us, life wants us to discover these answers because that is the purpose of human existence.

To understand life, learn how to live it and, in time, attain enlightenment, is what we are here for. Everything that happens to us, especially the outsize disasters and catastrophes, can be seen as a polite (or perhaps not so polite?) tap on our shoulder by life. "Are you sure you are going the right way?" it seems to ask us, adding, "Consider changing yourself." The smart ones may learn their lessons through one or two mistakes. Many others may need to face continuous drubbing before it dawns upon them that life is not going to change. It is they who will have to do that.

There is a surer way to laser through this fog of appearance and reality. I would say, meditate on happiness. Everywhere there is talk of happiness. It is the number one goal in everyone's lives. The American Constitution has even enshrined its pursuit as a basic human right. Closer home, the Indian scriptures proclaim that our essential nature is *sat-chit-ananda*: existence, consciousness and *bliss*! Our nature is to be blissful. Why not use this as a starting point to discover the truth of life? Great sages have stated this again and again. Maybe we can use this as a hypothesis, and set out to discover this inner happiness.

The first step is to really *want* to be happy. To enquire into it. This will draw it into our lives. This, at least, has been my experience. It was 1990. I had just become editor of *Society* magazine and I had never been more miserable in my life. In addition to the ongoing angst that had plagued me for years, there were additional reasons for misery, such as anxiety about my performance as an editor, my discomfort in a romantic relationship I had more or less been inveigled into, and a health challenge. Halfway through that memorable year, my very misery made me yearn to experience happiness. I longed to know what happiness felt like and where it was to be found. I looked around at all the people I knew to see if any of them could guide me. But no, they were just as confused as I was.

At that time I went to stay at a relative's house and found her and her three children locked in violent disputes. I shuddered at the misery experienced there which renewed my determination to find happiness. Six months later, on a cold January night, I got my awakening and all the answers unfolded.

What would meditating on happiness entail? It would mean studying people who are happy and looking at the way they behave, recognising their attitudes and examining their problem-solving methodologies. Happy people are the text we need to decipher in order to get access to the secret of happiness. The beauty of this methodology is that whatever you deeply study will infuse into you. This is the heart of *bhakti* yoga. This is why devotees spend hours praying to, washing, dressing and decorating their chosen deities. Since each of these deities is vested with certain qualities or characteristics; in time these qualities will seep into the devotee.

Reading texts and literature about happiness would also help you go deeper into the subject. It is most important to ponder about anything that has caught your notice either through the study of people or texts. Think about it. Turn it over in your mind. What gives X the capacity to be unruffled despite being subjected to a tirade by his boss? What makes Y sail through the serious illness of his father despite its demands on his time, energy and money? What gives Z that blithe spirit that rarely leaves her?

The more you think about it, the more you fertilise your quest for happiness. Sooner or later, the very inquiry will yield results.

It is a mistake to believe that our nature is given by God and that we can't do anything about it. Never believe that you are condemned to be morose and unhappy. Our nature is clay that we are meant to mould. Happy people have learnt to be happy, perhaps in this lifetime or an earlier one. If they can do it, so can we.

Once you have experienced true happiness, your life shifts radically. Your compass finally points North and all the confusion clears up. You never ever want to sacrifice that seraphic peace and harmony that steeps into you. And you realise that a prerequisite to happiness is a perfectly clear conscience. So you begin to work on your value system and strive for integration. You also begin to evaluate all your other goals and desires on the parameter of happiness. And you realise that for nothing on earth would you risk losing happiness, just for the sake of making money or ensnaring fame.

The choicest blessings of life, and the biggest of these is happiness, comes to us only through a pure heart. The worldly-wise may pride themselves on their smartness in business and their success in getting their way. They may amass a fortune, wield power or enjoy the adulation of millions, but the real blessings of life will elude them unless they purify their value system and overhaul their ethics. The wise Creator has instituted safeguards to ensure that no one can hammer at the gates of happiness without the entry pass of a peaceful conscience and a kind and giving heart.

After my awakening, the pursuit of absolute happiness became my Holy Grail. It put me on the path. I was determined to attain that wonderful state I had experienced for a year even if I had to die in pursuit of it.

The rest of my life has really all been about attaining this happiness. After I became more familiar with spiritual terminology, I discovered that what I meant by happiness was only another name for enlightenment.

My life has unfolded amazingly in the last 29 years. The years have not always been easy, but with every step I find myself moving ever closer to the goal of happiness.

The inquiry into happiness has given me everything I could ever want – a meaningful career, the love and gratitude of readers, enough money for my needs, the love of friends and family and good health.

Lesson #18

Growth Lies outside Your Comfort Zone

I have a friend who is locked in a toxic marriage. There is very little in common between her and her husband. He is suspicious of everyone who calls to speak to her, which, as a corporate lawyer, happens quite often. He controls both their accounts and scrutinises her every expenditure. She never tires of complaining about him, but she is unprepared to take the steps either to repair her marriage or walk out of it. "A known devil is better than an unknown one," she explains morosely.

Another friend has been in the same dead-end job for the last 25 years. He dreams of being an entrepreneur and would probably be able to swing it, but he dare not leave his job, for he has his mother, wife and two kids to feed. You can't blame him, but at the same time, his life is going nowhere and this brilliant man is now getting increasingly dispirited with his lot.

Growth lies out of our comfort zone. The two are polar opposites. Comfort zone is a lovely place to be in. It is great to loll around reading a good thriller or romantic novel, popping a chocolate into our mouths while reaching out for the remote to turn on our favourite show. But after a while, doesn't it pall? You chafe at the sameness of the thriller or the chocolate or the show. You chafe at the narrow, though safe, bounds of your comfort zone. You dream of doing exciting things. Perhaps learn a new language, travel to the Himalayas on your own, take up a new job, learn meditation or Reiki. And yet, when you think of the time, money or effort you have to invest, you simply slump even deeper into your comfort zone and clutch your remote with redoubled vigour.

There is a beautiful saying that goes something like this: "You have to let go of who you are, in order to become who you could be." I read this when I was on the threshold of a massive shift. I was about to jump into the process of deconditioning myself. Simply put, I was going to take a deep long look at what 16 years of depression had done to me, and heal myself of it. It was such a scary decision. Would I be able to cope with all that I was going to see of myself? How long would it take for me to heal? Who would I be in the interim? But this quote, God bless the writer, comforted and strengthened me enormously. I could become the person I was deep inside – strong, capable, loving and giving. I had to take the chance. I am so glad I did it. The years inbetween were often deeply unhappy, but they were meaningful. I was on a journey to my true self, and that made all the difficulties worthwhile.

It is never easy to get out of our comfort zone. All too often, our lack of confidence and inability to cope with challenges may prevent us from doing so. And it is important to listen to the voice that tells you that you are not ready as yet. There is no need to be rash and reckless. At the same time, can you consider equipping yourself to live life? I am still essentially a cautious person. I wonder at people who lead nomadic lives, or who begin to paint, learn to swim or develop a dozen other skills. I am not there yet. But all these years I have been working steadily on shedding my baggage, and building up my confidence and capabilities in order to free myself more and more of my comfort zone. As an introvert with poor social skills, being with others was often excruciatingly uncomfortable. But because of my constant inner work, today I find myself extremely comfortable with people to such an extent that people at my workshops often tell me that they feel deeply welcomed and at home in my presence.

As I have felt my confidence and capabilities increase, I have steadily expanded my capacity to leave my comfort zone. Many of the areas that once caused me acute discomfort, such as technology, or coping with change, or caregiving, come more easily to me now.

There was a time when I never let dominating people into my space because I could not cope with them. As my self-esteem grew, I gradually began to interact with them, though even now I have vestiges of uneasiness with them.

The one thing I have maintained as an article of faith is that the moment I am ready from within, I must do what I have hitherto hesitated to do. For I do not want to leave Planet Earth with the feeling that I did not do all that I was meant to.

The more we play safe, the more we play small, the more we dig deep into stuckness, the more we diminish as people. We will look around at other people, pelting along at the speed of light, writing books, building houses, travelling continents, winning awards, and wonder where our life went.

When you begin to flex your discomfort muscles, more opportunities open up. Instead of always opting for the easy option, you begin to explore the difficult ones. Instead of jumping into a cab, how about taking a bus or a train instead? Instead of ordering out each time your cook does not show up, how about cooking? Instead of whiling away your holidays, why not teach English to your maid's kids? Instead of putting some money into an envelope on your niece's birthday, how about a beautiful handmade gift?

At the end of the day, when you look back at all that you have become, you will have the ineffable satisfaction of knowing that your time on Planet Earth has been put to good use.

Lesson #19

It's All Your Stuff

The external orientation of our senses and mind is so pronounced that we almost always blame the outside world for our problems and for the way we feel about it. From tyrannical parents, competitive siblings and colleagues, unappreciative bosses and uncaring spouses, to unsupportive government policies and a downright cruel God, our lives always seem to be at the mercy of the other.

It is the crux of the spiritual approach that we gradually take the inquiry within and look to embrace our own culpability. The more we do that, the more we realise the magnitude of our own involvement. For me, one of the standout moments on this journey was the recognition that it is not what others do, say or act that bother us. *It is how we feel about these things that really gets to us.* In fact, I have crafted my own little mantra to encapsulate the learning. It goes thus: *What other people say, do or think is their stuff, and has nothing to do with me. How I feel about what they say, do or think is my stuff and has nothing to do with them.*

Think about it. Your mother nagging you to clean up your room may drive you ballistic, but it seems to be sweet music to your brother's ears. Two responses to the same stimulus. So how can we be bereft of responsibility in the matter? And what is it that upsets us so much about our mother's behaviour? For that, don't we need to look into our relationship with her, our relationship with ourselves, our level of self-esteem and so on?

In short, our every reaction will tell us where we need to work on ourselves so that we can get to the space where no matter what happens on the outside domain, our inner world will be serene and peaceful and our inner self will be lapping in a sea of peace.

Is that even possible? Indeed it is. For as we progress even deeper along the journey, one more layer unfolds and we recognise that *it is not even how we feel that really gets to us, it is how we resist what we feel.*

Interesting, isn't it? Take the inquiry within for a moment and explore for yourself what it would have been like if you were not to resist the anger that has been building inside of you ever since your maid had the effrontery to ask for a salary hike in spite of constant absenteeism and shoddy work? Without the resistance, your anger would have dissipated, for it is the nature of emotions to come and go. They get sticky when they find resistance towards them within us. Without the resistance, all that would remain would be a situation which you need to respond to.

That is so in all cases. It is our inability to withstand our feelings and thoughts that really puts us at their mercy.

So, is it easy to accept our feelings and thoughts and other aspects of our inner world? If it were, we would all be enlightened souls floating about Planet Earth with a blissful smile on our faces. Alas, it is not.

As someone who has been doggedly working on owning my stuff for the last couple of decades, I can testify that it is one of the hardest things on earth. But the more I work on myself, the more I progress. Bit by painful bit, it is getting gradually easier for me to get in touch with my feelings, thoughts, physical sensations and the resistance that I have for them.

Insights are showing up to guide me to the space where I can contain all the mind-stuff and not allow it to deflect me from the moment.

A few days ago, I had an Aha moment when I found myself affirming: Because I love myself unconditionally, I accept all my feelings, thoughts and physical sensations. To me that made enormous sense. Of course. The true proof of unconditional love is your capacity to accept everything about yourself. If you love yourself unconditionally, you can't leave even an atom of mind-stuff out in the cold. Even though none of it is ultimately who we are (because we are only what the Higher Self is – *sat-chit-ananda*), it still exists in our space and therefore needs to be embraced. For the first time, I feel that there is a reason for me to accept everything.

Recently, another little insight presented itself that is making me defuse my feelings and my resistance. I am recognising that I don't have to resist anything in my mind space because it is only by going through them that I will come to the other side. By going through thoughts, I will come to silence. By going through resistance, I will come to acceptance and by going through ill health, I will come to health. There is no reason to fear the mind-stuff or suppress it. It is what I need to go to the other side. How wonderful!

Recently, I had the experience of having a spiritual teacher holding a class on Buddhism come down on me like a ton of bricks when I asked her an innocuous question on whether we would be meditating or was the class only focussing on the teachings. Rattled though I was initially, I refused to engage with her beyond a point and stayed quite calm while she tried to browbeat, embarrass and mock me.

The reason I was able to do this was I kept telling myself that because I loved myself, I could accept everything I thought or felt. The thoughts and feelings flowed in and dissipated, exactly as if there were a drain from which they were oozing out.

It is making me recognise that if this keeps up, I will not need to be on guard with people. No matter how they show up, if I can hone my ability to accept my feelings, thoughts and physical sensations ongoingly, I will be unperturbed by their actions. As an extremely reactive and emotional person, such self-possession had always seemed like a dream. Along the path, I have always had insights and states of mind appear and disappear, almost as soon as I crow about them in print! So I am not taking any bets about how long this will last. Meanwhile, I shall continue working on myself.

Nevertheless, the prospect of finally owning my stuff, of not spraying my emotions out into an unwary world, of not letting myself down or putting myself in the wrong because of my hair-trigger reactions feels so much like liberation. I can hardly wait.

Lesson #20

Life Is a Happening

I was never a planner. In any case, from the age of 16 all the way to 32, I was so depleted by a mild but chronic state of depression that I had no space left for planning. So, life generally blew me around.

But even after I got my act together post my awakening, I spent little or no time in planning. I cannot really resonate with those who make watertight yearly, five-yearly and lifetime plans, chalked out with meticulous timelines for activity. This may work well when it comes to work goals over which you have some control, but life plans may be something else.

I have a young relative who had chalked out that she would get married at the age of 25, and have a couple of kids by the time she was 30. Naturally, she was most upset when the Universe refused to honour her plans and kept her waiting till 30 to get married.

However, the real disadvantage of over-planning is that we simply never allow the Universe room to work its magic. Maybe if we were not so set on going to Dubai for a holiday, a trip to Europe would have manifested. Maybe if we were not so determined to marry only a doctor, we might have married an ambassador. My point is, we need to hold our planning or expectations loosely, always willing for the Universe to topple it and send something else on its way.

This principle came stunningly to my notice when I spent a fortnight in London as part of a larger trip to North America, a farewell gift from my *Life Positive* publisher in 2017.

The friend who was to accompany me in London would be joining me only four days after I landed from New York. Fortuitously, the Universe was kind enough to send me a *sanyasi* friend of mine, who happened to be in London for the exact four days I was on my own.

Swamiji came to the apartment I was staying in punctually to pick me up the morning after I had arrived. We did not bother to plan our sightseeing and just stepped out, ready to embrace all of London. I saw a hedge bordering a park, and I told him that Nikhil (my friend's son, in whose house I was staying while he and his wife were holidaying in Mexico), had told me that their house was close to Hyde Park. Accordingly, we set off inside. After a walk in the beautiful park full of tall trees, thickly sprung with grass upon which pet dogs were tearing around, we came to a round lake full of swans and ducks. This was my first look at swans, who I had read about since childhood, and I was overjoyed to see these graceful birds first-hand.

We spent some time enjoying these beautiful birds and photographing them at various angles. Ahead we saw the Kensington Palace (where the young royals live), and deduced that we were in Kensington Park. After a look at a beautiful garden full of white flowers that were bordering the palace, we wandered on. Close by, we saw an imposing statue of Prince Albert, then crossed the road and went into the iconic Royal Albert Hall, the premier place for music concerts. Later, we went down the road and entered another filled with museums, including the Victoria and Albert Museum and the Science Museum. In half a day without any kind of planning, Swamiji and I had seen so much. And each sighting had seemed such a gift.

During both the days that we went sightseeing, it appeared as if God had planned our itinerary. Serendipity abounded. Since we both had tight budgets, we were delighted when we went to St Paul's Cathedral and found that we could enter for absolutely free if there were a Church service. To our luck, one was about to begin the moment we reached there.

At Westminster Abbey, Swamiji was let in for free because he was a monk, and I got a good concession because I was a senior citizen! Later, I mentioned to Swamiji in passing that I would have loved to see 10 Downing Street, the prime minister's official residence. Walking towards Trafalgar Square, we saw a crowd gathered around a particular building and, lo and behold, it was 10 Downing Street. We even got to see Teresa May's vehicle gliding by!

As a matter of fact, it does not take you long to recognise that most of the significant turning points in your life happen on their own. For instance, I got my job as editor of *Society* magazine because I had interviewed the publisher of Magna, Mr Nari Hira, a few months ago for *GFQ*, part of the *Gentleman* stable of magazines. The normally reclusive Mr Hira had agreed to the interview only because *TV and Video World*, another magazine from the *Gentleman* group, had taken the idea of a magazine based on the TV industry from him when he had sent around a brochure announcing the launch of *Showtime*. They had recently approached him for an interview. He refused, but to drive home the point, he had agreed to the *GFQ* interview! On such slender threads does destiny hang.

Again, my joining *Life Positive* had nothing to do with me. I had met the founding editor, Parveen Chopra, four months earlier while I was working on a prototype for a spiritual magazine for the Magna group, and Parveen was writing a book on the New Age movement in India. I quit Magna when it was decided to pull out the magazine because it was unlikely to make money. Miraculously, the very day I put in my papers, without anything in hand except a diehard determination to write only about spirituality, and no longer work for the mainstream media, Parveen called me to tell me that he was starting a body-mind-spirit magazine and was looking for a correspondent in Mumbai!

Significant friendships happened just like that, not because I set out to make them happen. Insights happened and I had nothing to do with them. My spiritual awakening, the biggest gift that God has given me, dropped on my lap like a ripe fruit. I was no seeker. I had no concept of spirituality. And yet, when my time came, I was anointed with an awakening. Life is a happening. There are much vaster forces in life than our own small self that set in motion the events of our lives. Karma is one such player. God's grace is another. Both these are beyond the control of the conscious mind. What is meant to come to us will come to us, as sure as the sun rises. What is not meant to come to us will not come, even if we try our heads off. That does not mean we do not try – but that we hold our intentions spaciously, knowing that the effort is ours but the fruit is God's domain.

Lesson #21

Things Get Better

How many times have we been through situations that seem irresolvable, and through crises that seem irreversible, such as a life despaired of, financial bankruptcy or the breakdown of a valuable relationship? And then, just like in the movies or books, something happens to resolve the situation and things get back to being better.

There have been many occasions in my own life when serious illnesses threatened to completely disable me – and yet here I am, still with my limbs and senses active (touch wood). I recall the time when I had an attack of rheumatoid arthritis, which is one of the most painful and debilitating forms of arthritis. Most people end up bedridden or wheelchair-ridden under its stinging attack. It began with my little finger in my left hand turning red, swollen and so painful that even a bump in an auto would send waves of pain through it. Then my other little finger followed suit. Then the ring fingers. Then my Venus mount began throbbing and hurting. My knees went next. I was horrified and petrified. Allopathy has no solution for the condition except to medicate you with steroids. After having dodged the ailment for years, was I finally going to go under? How would I earn my living, and look after my mother?

With little hope, I approached an Ayurvedic doctor I had newly met. Nonchalantly, he gave me some oil to drink (he called it liver oil – i.e., oil for the liver) and told me I would be fine in four days. I could hardly believe my ears. "Are you sure, doctor?" I asked him, doubtfully. "It's a question of my life." He waved me off cheerfully. I started drinking the oil and, sure enough, I could see the redness and the swelling begin to recede. In four days, my digits returned to their normal size and I was free!

Later on, I developed such a severe case of Irritable Bowel Syndrome (IBS) that I could digest virtually nothing. I lost weight precipitately because I could hardly eat any food. For nights at a stretch, I would skip dinner, hoping to pacify my recalcitrant stomach, but a year went by and I was no better. This left me so distressed and distraught that I actually reached a state where I contemplated suicide. But then slowly, after a couple of years, I began to improve. (Chapter 7 gives you a more comprehensive account of the healing, if you are interested). The tide turned, and I began the upswing. If you had asked me a few months before if I would ever heal, I honestly would not have been able to say yes. I often thought in my darker moments that I was doomed to go through this problem for life.

Has this not happened to you, too? At some point, imperceptibly, the upward rise begins. The illness wanes, the financial downswing stabilises and moves up, the irretrievable relationship suddenly starts to thaw, the writer's block lifts, and life begins to look up. A friend of mine was despairing for her father's life. It seemed just a matter of time before he would go, and then the next thing I knew, he was completely fine.

Another friend was locked in a contentious relationship with his mother and sister, and never expected it to get better. But in the fullness of time, the relationship improved and the family was able to mend its frayed bonds.

This seems to be a pattern with life. Things generally get better over time. Perhaps it has to do with the very nature of life itself. As the Buddha said, impermanence is at its core. So, good times come and go, and bad times come and go.

Or it just might have something to do with the healing power of time. Over time, things generally settle down. Unforgiveable wrongs mellow down into acceptable misdemeanours. How many parents, who had thrown their children out of their houses for having married someone of their choice, melt and relent when grandchildren gurgle and coo at them?

Or could it have something to do with the nature of life itself, which somehow prevails over all negative forces and spirals up?

It may have to do with our karma, too. At some point, perhaps we void that particular karma that gave us the issue, and somehow we surface. Above all, perhaps it is the grace of God that watches over us and compassionately extends a forgiving hand.

How many of us have nursed a broken heart and believed that the aching void in our chests would plague us forever? Yet, over time, the memory of the loved one grows faint, our heart heals, happiness steals back and we notice gladly the sunrays slanting over the leaves, the cool breeze rustling through our hair and the love in our mother's eyes.

This really ought to give us great comfort. More often than not, the dreaded denouement does not happen. From somewhere, redemption comes.

I cannot think of the number of times the meteorological department sighted a cyclone hovering around Mumbai and issued stern warnings. All of us battened down our hatchets and waited breathlessly for the storm to break but, happily, after having lived for over 40 years in Mumbai, I still cannot remember a single cyclone hitting the city. Inevitably, it veered off elsewhere, usually into the sea, and spared the megapolis.

So, even when the situation seems dire, never give up hope. Keep doing and keep praying, and surrender the situation to God. Remember that it is darkest before dawn.

Lesson #22

LIFE IS A PROCESS

How many books have you read in which the hero or the heroine falls in love, but does not marry the beloved either because the loved one marries someone else or suddenly dies tragically post the wedding? For the rest of their lives, the said hero/heroine lives in thrall to the person, never marrying again or even allowing themselves to be happy. Miss Havisham in Charles Dickens's *Great Expectations,* is a great example of this. Fantastically enough, she stopped all the clocks, and sat in her wedding gown surrounded by mouldering heaps of the wedding feast around her for the rest of her life! Many of us believe that we will never heal from the wounds life deals us. Many of us also believe that if we allow our memories to fade of the love we had for the beloved, even 10 years later, we are being unfaithful to them.

If only these people had allowed themselves to heal, they would have got a second chance at love and happiness.

A good number of us try our hand at public speaking or business or living alone. We may fail at it and scurry back to our old ways, swearing to never try this again. Now, I used to be a terrible speaker. I was shy, I was under-confident and I had a terrible habit of freezing with fear whenever I was invited to speak somewhere. Logically, I should have crawled under a rock and stayed there for the rest of my life.

But I was determined to be a good speaker. So, I simply never missed an opportunity, turned up and bravely made an ass of myself until I gradually became more confident. I will probably never be the best speaker in the business but, today, I am pretty confident about holding my own in the speaking world. And once I began to work as a facilitator, I was really grateful for my speaking smarts. It has helped me carve out a new career for myself.

So, let's remember that life is all about second chances. Simply because we have failed once, does not mean we should write ourselves off. We need to forgive ourselves and develop the courage to try again. And again. Until we get it right.

Life is a process, my dear friends. Unless we recognise that, we are going to short-change ourselves and the endless possibilities we are meant to realise. Success arises out of a series of failures. Good relationships happen through failing, falling and ceaselessly trying. All couples will tell you that life was pretty stormy in the early years of their marriage. What can you expect, after all, when two people of different sexes, backgrounds, often communities, castes and cultures, likes and dislikes decide to live together for the rest of their lives? It is never easy. Successful marriages happen only if both couples hold firmly to their commitment and keep returning to it after every blow-up. Success at work is also not a given. It takes grit and commitment day in and day out, with a good dollop of luck, to ensure that we finally reach our goals, both as entrepreneurs or as executives.

Parenting is another enterprise that takes any amount of attempts to get it right. Losing weight is a process, too.

Spiritual growth is another area where you will always have to remind yourself that it is a process. Let's face it. The person we show up to be, and the person we really are, can often be worlds apart. Take me, for example. When I stepped on the path about 29 years ago, I was in a sorry state. My memory, focus, concentration, self-control, self-esteem and so many other things were all shot to bits. I was a combustible cocktail of fear, worry, anxiety, anger, panic and many other negatives. It took a real act of imagination to believe that I had any chance of becoming a Buddha or a Ramana Maharshi. All I had was a staunch determination that come hell or high water, death or devastation, I was simply going to walk the path, one step at a time. I have not got there yet but, once in a while, I think back on the person I was, and the person I presently am, and am pleasantly surprised. I have indeed transformed myself. Not fully, perhaps. But hugely.

Life is a dynamic interplay of opposites. Success emerges out of failure and, unless we are careful, failure emerges from success. Joy lies in the heart of sadness and vice versa. So, never give up. That is the only thing you need to do to finally win in this enterprise called life. No matter how many times you go down, get up and try at it again.

I admit that this is not easy. If only we could go to a store and buy the courage and confidence we need to fuel our resilience. But worry not, my friends. These qualities are within us. And accessing them is nothing but a process. It consists of accepting the many times you may not have demonstrated these qualities, forgiving yourself for that and recommitting yourself to live by them.

Everything is a process. This is the truth. So, get back into the game. It does not matter how far back you are. If you never give up, you, too, have a chance of winning, like anyone else.

Lesson #23

KARMA AND REINCARNATION ARE REAL

Let's face it. Until we acquaint ourselves with the concept of karma, life makes absolutely no sense. One of the main reasons for many of us to spin away from religion is because the world as we see it is profoundly unjust, not to mention arbitrary. How do you explain why some people are bone poor, while others hardly know what to do with their money? Why are some people born with perfect health, while others are born blind, deaf or lame? And yet others have to contend with autism, Down's Syndrome and other dreadful mental afflictions? Why does life always favour some people while consistently sending disasters to others? Why does success woo a few, only to ignore the others? Unless one is content with the concept of a whimsical God who rewards or punishes as She pleases, it simply does not make sense. And, considering the intrinsic order and harmony of this beautiful Universe, where planets move in their orbit, where season gives way to season and night follows day predictably, it is an insult to anyone's concept of God to imagine that we would be this short-changed.

Only karma explains the world fully and enables us to comprehend its beautiful, just and perfect design. So, what is karma? Its simplest and clearest definition comes from the Bible, even though, ironically, its followers do not subscribe to the karma theory! "As you sow, so shall you reap," it says with admirable brevity in Galatians 6:7.

There are consequences to everything we think, speak or do. There are consequences to the motivation behind all of them. Thus using a knife to cut open a watermelon, and using it to kill someone, have different consequences. Giving charity because you really want to help, and giving charity because it elevates you in society, will have different consequences. These consequences will eventually determine our destiny, not just in this lifetime but in all the others. We have taken birth in this lifetime to void the karma that has ripened, and every significant aspect of our present life owes its design to karma. The country we are born in, the language we speak, the family we belong to, our appearance, our talents, our personality, have all been determined by karma.

This also means that karma and reincarnation are inextricably linked. One cannot exist without the other, for we cannot possibly void all our karmas in one lifetime. Many take lifetimes to ripen. In this regard, consider the case of Dhritarashtra (the blind king and head of the Kuru clan, from the Mahabharata). The loss of his 100 sons during the Great War is attributed to the fact that aeons before, he had once killed the 100 cygnets of a swan's family. It took him countless lifetimes to earn sufficient merit to deserve 100 sons, and it was only then that his karma could play out.

So complex and subtle are the ways of karma that it is impossible for us to trace all its consequences, though many ripen immediately. We trip over someone's shoe and we fall. We feel hungry and we eat. We eat too well and get a stomach upset. But other karmas, such as thefts, treason, cheating or rape, or saving a life, serving society selflessly, sacrificing our life to save another, may ripen in this lifetime or may be carried on to another lifetime.

This can explain why dreadful things or windfalls happen to us without prior warning. Suddenly, you might find yourself in an accident, or accused and may be imprisoned for something you have not done or smitten by a serious illness. Likewise, you might find yourself winning the lottery, falling in love and marrying your soulmate, or getting the job of your dreams. In either case, never ask yourself what you have done to deserve it. In some distant past of your immortal life, you would have carefully stored up the good or bad karma that is presently visiting you.

Many consider karma to be a fatalistic concept; one which militates against the concept of free will. But that arises out of a faulty understanding of the term. If karma arises out of our thoughts, words and deeds, it means that only we are the determinants of our destiny. There is no impersonal fate or God who writes it for us. Therefore, it means we alone have power over our lives. Thus, if we have earned an unfortunate karma for ourselves, the patience, wisdom and commitment with which we endure our *tapasya*, as well as the dynamism, resourcefulness and intelligence with which we work our way out of it, will help us build a better karma for ourselves that will eventually take us out of the hole.

So, the thing to do when bad karma hits us is two-fold. First, we earn as much good karma as we can by not cribbing about it, by accepting it, making the most of it and also using it to help others. Secondly, we try our damndest to learn the lessons it holds for us. What did we do wrong that we fell so badly ill, or lost our job or our sweetheart? How can we make sure that the problem does not revisit us? If we learn our lessons and change our behaviour, the problem will not return. Otherwise, it will.

The more we learn to think, say and do the right thing, the better our karma. The only way to free ourselves of karma is to live according to the laws of the Universe.

Karma is the swift kick in the pants we get when we violate these laws. Thus, every time something goes wrong with our lives, such as flubbing a test or failing in our business enterprise, it is a good thing to look back and see how we have drawn it to us. Have we been fearful of this eventuality? Have we been thinking about our welfare and not that of others? Have we been ethical in our operations? The more questions we ask, the more likely we are to find out our stumbling block and correct it. Thus, through the agency of karma, we get a chance to rectify our errors and move forward with greater awareness and attentiveness.

There is much more to karma than the few pointers I have mentioned here. I must also tell you that there are three forms of karma: *sanchita* karma, *prarabdh* karma and *agami* karma. *Sanchita* karma is the sum total of our karma, while *prarabdh* karma refers to the karma that has ripened in this lifetime and which determines our destiny. *Agami* karma is the karma we are shaping at this moment through our thoughts, words and deeds.

Now, if we keep making fresh karma, how on earth are we ever to reach the stage when we become free of karma, thereby spelling an end to the cycle of birth and death?

The design of life is indeed ingenious, and the Creator's intelligence knows no bounds. The moment we have an enlightenment experience, the whole sack of *sanchita* karma dissolves and disappears. We are left only with our present karma – *prarabdh*. And when that is dissolved and we have learnt to free ourselves of all base motivations, or even good ones, we reach the stage of *nishkama* karma of which the Bhagavad Gita tells us. Dispassionate action based on the welfare of the whole, and not driven by personal motivation, will not earn us any karma. We will be like a bird that flies without leaving any trace.

Then and then alone will we attain enlightenment and therefore earn our freedom from the cycle of birth and death.

Lesson #24

Void Your Karma Speedily

One of my favourite stories revolves around a king and a queen who were visited by God. "Some bad karma is part of your destiny," said the Lord. "Would you rather take it now or delay it?" The king and his queen conferred and, being wise, they decided that they would rather face the karma when they were young and healthy than wait until the debilities of old age added to the difficulty. Accordingly, a neighbouring king invaded their kingdom, and the king, queen and their son were exiled into a forest. Years passed, the son grew up and, pretty soon, he managed to free the kingdom from the invader and take back the reins. The king and queen led the end of their lives in the comfort of the palace and the care of a loving son.

This is wisdom. Alas, most of us would rather keep pushing the karma further and further into the future, and living it up presently. We drink, smoke or eat unwisely, damaging our health. When karma strikes back, instead of heeding it, we continue our merry way until it is too late and cancer or some horrible ailment ensnares us.

We know we should mend our relationship with our mother-in-law, sibling or spouse, but we keep putting it off until the day the relationship explodes, plunging us into deep sorrow. We know we should live within our means, but the lure of the credit card and the number of goodies on the shop window keep enticing us, until the day when we find our money gone and an indigent future beckoning us.

The smartest possible thing we can do is to void our karma the moment it presents itself to us. When relationships go wrong, can we mend them by seeing where we have gone wrong and making amends?

The sooner we learn our lessons and apply them to the process of living, the happier will the rest of our lives get. But, of course, this is never easy. The ego wants the easy way out – pleasure and a good life. It does not want to suffer and, therefore, ultimately ends up suffering a lot more.

When I moved on to the path of spirituality about 29 years ago, and decided to take stock of my personality and work on healing myself of all the wounds and dents that had been dealt to it, I knew it was not going to be pleasant. Indeed, it is excruciating to see your shadow side up close. But I was determined that I would face it and dissolve it, for there was no other way to be free. Those years were intensely painful, but they were also meaningful and interspersed with moments of joy and laughter. I was finally living and moving towards a better future. Above all, I finally understood life, and was able to live it right side up.

With every year, I have felt my baggage grow lighter. Around 2014, I felt a definite loosening of my karma. That year went wonderfully well for me. Everything was coming up roses. The last of the big karmas that had confronted me was the Irritable Bowel Syndrome. After it gradually became manageable, every year has only been better and better.

In 2015, I began my writer's workshops, which, by the grace of God, became quite popular. After many years of living on a tight budget, I found that abundance had finally come my way. Every astrologer I had ever met had predicted that I would never make money. The fact that I am making enough and maybe a little more than I need, is proof that whatever karmic pattern had blocked money from my destiny has now healed.

There was a time when I had felt myself tied by invisible cords that prevented me from any action. This to me is what karma feels like. All the limitations we labour under are the sum total of our karma. The freer we are from restrictive circumstances, the freer we are of karma. If we are still limited by contentious relationships, poor health, difficult finances, a toxic work environment, then understand that we are still under the power of karma.

In my case, most of those cords that once bound me are slowly loosening. I feel relatively free, though, of course, there is no way of saying if more karma is coming my way. If it does assail me, I am willing to face it. I have come to terms with the fact that this lifetime is all about voiding my karmas. And why not? After all, I am working towards eternity, so, one lifetime of suffering is a small price to pay for an eternity of happiness and peace.

Lesson #25

Focus on What Is Permanent

Once we delve into the mysteries of life and death, and recognise the truth of karma and reincarnation, we also understand that we are immortal. Our soul, which also includes our psyche or our mind, is immortal. It is only the body that dies with each birth. When the body dies, our immaterial and immortal remains move on to the after-life.

Now, according to all that I have read, the soul is whole and perfect and does not change. It is the domain of the Higher Self. The psyche or the mind, however, changes according to the use we have put of our lives on Planet Earth. If we have used our lives to grow as human beings, then our psyche would have evolved. If we have misused our lives to bring misery to ourselves and others, our psyche would have regressed. If we have neither used it for the good or for the bad, then it would have stagnated. If that is so, should that not be our area of focus in this lifetime, since it is the only thing that outlasts death?

And since every human has an immortal soul and psyche, it follows that relationships, too, will outlast death. A record of the state of every relationship will be inscribed on our psyche. Whom we loved, assisted, healed, hated, abused, manipulated, ignored and so on. Our karmic balance sheet will, for the most part, revolve around our relationships. Therefore, that, too, is something we must prioritise. *In sum, there are only two things worth cultivating in a mortal body – our personal growth and our relationships.*

What does personal growth mean? We are here to grow as human beings. We are meant to rise above every limitation we labour under. We are meant to increase and perfect our stores of joy, love, compassion, competence, capability, intelligence, wisdom, strength, power, honesty, courage, balance and discipline. Another and more accurate way of putting this is that we must eliminate the illusion that we are weak, cowardly, indifferent, incompetent, stupid, unhappy and undisciplined. The truth is that we are Soul, and the soul is whole and perfect. It is always the embodiment of all positive qualities. But we identify with our self-created personality which is the sum total of all the conditioning we have picked up in the journey of lifetimes. When we dismantle this false personality, our soul will shine forth.

Even though it is easy to write it, it is quite simply the hardest thing in the world to eliminate our personality, for it requires deep inner work. We need to be able to face ourselves as we truly are. We need to cultivate the courage to admit our faults and face our shadow self. The work would also include healing from the wounds of the past, overcoming the fears of the future and coming to rest in the present moment.

This work is the most imperative task we have on Planet Earth. We are not here only to study, get a job, get married, have children and exit the planet. We are here to become better human beings because the end goal of the human enterprise is simply this: Enlightenment. We are meant to fully free ourselves of our false personality and ego, which will automatically cause our real Self to shine forth. This Self is the God part of us, the Soul. When we have achieved this massive, momentous and excruciating task, we will be free from the cycle of birth and death. We will no longer be required to take human incarnation. We will move on to more evolved civilisations. Of course, many return, driven by compassion for the fallen mankind that looks everywhere for answers to the mystery of life, but never looks within, where only it exists.

The second task is to cultivate our relationships so that each of them is healthy. Healing stuck or negative relationships will take the most work. What we need to remember is that unless we heal these relationships, they will keep coming back lifetime after lifetime, until we resolve our issues with them. And since we are looking to free ourselves of further lifetimes, it is imperative that we heal each relationship as soon as we can. Furthermore, if we find that their behaviour is unforgivable, we need to recognise that perhaps we have drawn it through equally unforgivable behaviour in some other lifetime. It is absolutely true that we have drawn every single event in our lives, big and small, positive or negative, through our own actions in this or some other lifetime.

So let's buckle down and resolve our relationships, for they alone are the source of our greatest joy and deepest sorrow. The relationships that need the greatest amount of work would be with our immediate family, for we would have spent several lifetimes playing different roles and creating deep karmic imbalances. They are also the most difficult, for the baggage we carry in each of them will be immense. Deep patient work, a commitment to resolving it regardless of the other, and God's grace will help us work through it.

The greatest amount of karma we incur in each lifetime is with our parents. There is simply no way we can ever repay them for all that they do. Therefore, seize every opportunity to serve your parents and do good to them, for you cannot hope to get self-realisation without setting that balance straight.

I did virtually nothing for my father when he was stricken with a brain tumour and passed away in a few months, so

I have to just hope that perhaps the scales were settled in some other lifetime. But when my mother was felled by a stroke and rendered paralysed for the last two-and-a-half years of her life, I was her chief caregiver, since she lived with me. While my sister, Susan, also shared the burden of caregiving, the responsibility for her welfare was mine. My mother had looked after me virtually till her fatal illness. Her illness gave me a chance to care for her, too, and after her death, my life opened up considerably. In the years that I was looking after her, I had asked for and got a better salary so my finances were better. Moreover, I had refurbished my house and felt privileged to live in a beautiful apartment. And my spiritual growth accelerated. I attribute all of these blessings to the fact that, clearly, some major karma had been settled with the passage of my mother.

If in each lifetime we focus only on our growth and the health of our relationships, we will grow in quantum leaps. Of course, this means freeing ourselves of our endless preoccupation with the mortal body – how it looks, how to clothe it, feed it, house it, pleasure it. It also means recognising the futility of desire for money, fame, power and status. These things will not accompany us beyond the grave. We must leave them all behind. How foolish to waste our precious human lives in pursuits that will not ultimately benefit us.

Lesson #26

Find Yourself

Truly, the whole purpose of this enterprise called Life is to enable us to become our own person. By this I mean, freeing ourselves from the undue influence or power of others, and learning to think and act for ourselves. It also means cultivating a code of conduct and a value system from which we seldom swerve, thus giving us a clearly discernible character. To begin with, as children we barely have any power, nor do we have a clear idea of who we are. Our parents, or our teachers and sometimes our peers, overpower us and govern our thinking, belief systems, actions and behaviour.

But maturity is really all about building our capacity to pull away from society's influence and giving free rein to our own authentic nature. I personally believe that I was born with a tattoo on my head that read, "Don't tell me what to do." Nevertheless, I found it hard to say it to anyone since I was an under-confident, shy kid whom anyone could boss around, and many did.

But where it really counted, in my mind, I was pretty independent and capable of taking radical decisions even at an early age. My first move away from the common herd was to stop believing in God at the age of 14. I have mentioned this in an earlier chapter so will not elaborate on it, save that for a Christian to give up faith is considered heresy.

My second radical decision is not something I can talk about without putting many others in a bad light, but suffice it to say that almost everyone, including my mother, urged me to take an action that would benefit me in my board exams, but which was not ethical. After a hard day's tussle with my conscience I decided to not do so, even though I was the only one to stand against it. It was one of the hardest decisions I had taken in my 16 years of life, but the strength I derived from it was unparalleled.

Even though my youth was submerged in depression, and my presence did not really shine out until my spiritual awakening set me straight, I rarely did the wrong thing and, usually, had my own ideas about life. For instance, despite being deeply idealistic, I was never attracted to communism or feminism, which were burning topics when I was growing up in the '70s. I could not have said why, but neither subject attracted me. It was as if something in me was wired to respond to nothing less than a spiritual shake-up. Instinctively, I could see the limitations of communism and the anti-male stance of feminism. Today, I would call myself a feminist but one who is pro women, and not anti-men as feminists were at that time.

The drive towards becoming my own person accelerated only after my spiritual awakening, for it organised everything for me and helped me understand all of life. Best of all, it gave me the parameters to take decisions, which I was hopeless at earlier, and enabled me to arrive at my own independent value system of right and wrong.

When it came to decisions, at least major ones, I simply abided by my inner voice, whose presence I became conscious of only then. I realised the folly of decisions arrived at through the head and, instead, chose to abide by the gut. My voice has thus far always led me right, even when I made major decisions such as jumping out of the editorship of *Society* magazine without a job in hand in 1996, when the conflict between the values I practised and believed in and the values I was propagating through *Society* became too glaring to ignore. Fortunately, a merciful Universe caught me in a safety net that very evening through a job with *Life Positive*.

Other decisions like taking over the editorship of *Life Positive*, or starting my writer's workshops or leaving *Life Positive*, were also undertaken under the advice of the inner voice.

As for my value system, now that I knew that happiness was the highest priority, and that one could only arrive at it through focussing on the happiness of others, it became clear to me that anything that added to the sum total of planetary or even universal happiness was right, and anything that detracted from it was wrong.

Earlier, I had instinctively known that lying, stealing, inflicting violence, abusing another, was wrong, but I could not explain why. Now I understood that since these acts destroyed another's happiness, they were not in humanity's best interests. Simultaneously, helping a blind person cross the road, financing the education of your domestic help's children, coming to the aid of someone being physically assaulted, cleaning up the beaches of Mumbai, were all laudable acts because they helped increase universal happiness.

All this gave me tremendous clarity and a certain confidence in my own capacity to understand and make my way through life. I seldom ask others for advice on what to do, unless it concerns practical matters such as which mobile or laptop to buy, because I would rather go by my own gut.

As I became more confident of the merit of my own value system, I became pretty much a non-conformist. Not a rebel, for I was never interested in protesting, but a quiet non-conformist who did what her conscience or her principles prompted her to do, whether or not it aligned with society's notions.

For starters, I totally rejected society's obsession with money, fame, power and possessions, because I could see clearly that they were taking us away from growth and the pursuit of happiness. Having left the prestigious *Society* magazine for a start-up like *Life Positive*, I had anyway turned my back to the material life, and I joyously carved out a minimalistic life for myself where the only luxury I allowed myself was to write only about holistic matters.

I steer clear of buying more and more or new and improved as much as possible. For me, old is gold and I hold on to my possessions as long as I can. I also do not believe in owning multiples of possessions. I usually use only one pair of shoes, bag or watch at a time, and buy the next only after the present one has worn itself out.

I also moved more and more away from the pull of mass consciousness that has most of us in its thrall. No advertisement can ever convince me to buy a product that I don't need simply because others are buying it. I do not follow fashion trends unless they agree with my sense of aesthetics and ethics. I do not subscribe to the present fashion of wearing torn clothes, because I think in a country like India where millions wear torn clothes because they have no choice, it is extremely insensitive to make such clothing a fashion statement

I watch little television save for movies and funny shows. I completely avoid the news, both in print and on TV, for I do not want to flood my system with fear and negativity.

This is as far as I have got. I look forward to seeing how my inner me grows and expresses herself in the future.

Lesson #27

Take Off Your Masks

I once read an enchanting book called *The Velveteen Rabbit* about a little toy rabbit much beloved by its owner, who was given the secret of becoming real by a fellow toy – a Skin Horse. "When a child loves you for a long, long time, not just to play with, but REALLY loves you, then you become Real," said the wise horse.

He continues: "It doesn't happen all at once. You become. It takes a long time. That's why it doesn't happen often to people who break easily, or have sharp edges, or who have to be carefully kept. Generally, by the time you are Real, most of your hair has been loved off, and your eyes drop out and you get loose in the joints and very shabby. But these things don't matter at all, because once you are Real you can't be ugly, except to people who don't understand."

Can we not resonate with the profound truth these words express? And is our own human journey all that different from the toy rabbit's?

We, too, are on the path to becoming real. And why it is so difficult is that it takes us such a long time to realise that we are not real! This is true of us at many levels but, at the immediate level, it speaks to us of the many masks we hide under, because we are so afraid that who we are is not enough. We put on an American accent without ever leaving India because we hope that it will give us a higher status among our peers. In our teens, we indulge in so many self-destructive activities like smoking or drinking, just to fit in with our peers.

I once read the real-life story of someone who was, at heart, a shy, sensitive introverted youth. But his father was an up-by-the-bootstraps sort of person who wanted his boys to be strong and manly, afraid of nothing and carrying the world before them. So, the boy dutifully reinvented himself to fit that image. In time, he became a famous pastor with millions of followers. And then, one day, the bubble burst when he was found cheating on his wife. From the rubble of his former life, this man then began to dig for his true self, hidden so deeply under his flamboyant extroverted image that it took him years.

Many of our most outstanding achievers will tell you that their chief motivation was a desperate need to disprove their belief that they were not good enough.

Who we are is a mystery to even the most perceptive among us. Our moods, feelings, impulses and instincts seem to move us in a way we cannot control. More than half the time, we are left looking open-mouthed as these imposters cause us to say and behave in ways that do not have our sanction. As if that is not bad enough, everyone has an opinion on how we should be. From our earliest age, our parents, siblings and, later, our teachers, are perennially moulding and shaping our behaviour and, eventually, our image of who we are. Someone calls us a bad boy or bad girl and, for the rest of our lives, we either act out this badness or compensate for it by trying to be the soul of virtue.

Eventually, who we take ourselves to be is the sum total of all that others and we ourselves have thought of ourselves. For instance, I used to think of myself as an extremely lazy, moody and difficult person. I am still not done with dismantling this image, though I have long been convinced that this is not my true self.

For most of us, the journey to becoming real includes developing confidence in ourselves and cultivating a sturdy self-esteem. When we can love and appreciate ourselves and believe in our innate worth, we can take the risk of coming out of hiding and becoming the person we truly are. It is okay to cry in a movie. We don't have to be macho if that is not who we are. It is okay to not know how to use a fork and knife. We don't have to pretend to be sophisticated. It is okay to lose it sometimes. We don't have to pretend to be strong.

Gradually, we become the same person in all situations and with everyone. Even when we are alone with ourselves. We no longer think of dialogues and stories to tell others. We no longer want to impress anyone. We no longer dress for effect. We slowly sink into our skin, and become comfortable in it.

The one thing that can help us hugely in this journey, as the Skin Horse said, is love. If we are fortunate enough to be loved unconditionally by someone – a parent, a spouse, a friend – then that helps us see ourselves as lovable and permits us to embrace ourselves. I was extremely fortunate to have a mother who loved me unconditionally. That love has, time and again, redeemed me, given me faith in myself, helped me to forgive myself and get back on my feet. I recall that for a whole year, a very challenging year, I had not gone home to Vizag, nor called her. Eventually, when I did go home, I was filled with guilt at my behaviour and wondered if my mother would ever forgive me. But her motherly love was vast enough to embrace me fully without even a passing reference to my shameful neglect of her and, therefore, I was able to forgive myself and resume the relationship.

At many points in my life, I have had the huge gift of unconditional acceptance, trust or forgiveness and, each time, I felt transformed by it. When I joined *Society* magazine as a rookie editor, I was terrified of failure, never having been an editor and having always shied away from responsibilities. But my publisher, Mr Nari Hira, simply offered me his total trust and respect. He had no doubt I had it in me to succeed. That trust and respect infused me with confidence and I slowly wobbled to my feet.

Whether through someone else's love or our own, the truth is, it is ultimately love that redeems us.

Lesson #28

Find Your Balance

Through all our ceaseless strife on the path, the place we eventually hope to reach is one of perfect balance. Today, each of us, and perhaps humanity itself, on the whole, is at a place in our evolution where we are asked to balance out all our polarities. At the gender level, we are asked to balance our yin and yang. Men need to enhance their feminine qualities, and women need to increase their masculine qualities.

I, for instance, was an extreme yin. Very regressive, passive, submissive, non-confrontationist, had poor boundaries and was a classic victim. Through a series of relationships whose only purpose appeared to be to help me balance this out, I learnt to become more assertive, dynamic and better at protecting my boundaries.

Since everything in the Universe is made up of the five elements (*panchamahabhootas* in Sanskrit), we need to examine where we stand with regard to each of them. These elements are earth, fire, water, air and space. When I made an inventory in the early stages of my spiritual journey, I discovered that I had way too much water and air, and very little of earth and fire. Space, apparently, was the only element I did not have an issue with. And perhaps that was because I could not understand too well how it translated into my personality! I was, therefore, sodden and stagnant, as well as spaced out. I had so little fire in me that I could hardly get myself to do anything, and my lack of earth quality made me feel extremely ungrounded. To set this balance right has been the journey of a lifetime. It was only through years and years of patient awareness and acceptance of all that showed up in my mind space that I gradually found myself able to take decisions, to act on decisions, to pay my bills on time, to get a haircut when I needed one and so on, instead of postponing everything endlessly. I still have a long way to go in this domain, but as I keep healing, I am sure the balance will be attained.

The other important balance for all of us is to balance the left brain and the right brain, and thus arrive at the whole brain. As in everything else, in this zone also I was an extreme case, being almost entirely a right brain with so little left brain faculties that I found it almost impossible to lead my life. I had, for instance, very little focus, concentration, will power, discipline, sense of organisation and order. Everything around me was in a constant state of flux and confusion. Papers were strewn around without any order, I could never remember the tasks I had to do and, therefore, forgot to do them, and my racing mind almost never let up or stopped. I was always behindhand in all that I had to do, and time was a tyrant, relentlessly prodding me to get a move on. This, too, has taken me decades of patient trawling before I could reach some semblance of efficiency and competence, even though I still feel I have a long way to go before I can get to the calm order and competence that others seem to command so effortlessly.

This is one balance that is valid for the human race as a whole. The East is essentially right-brained, and the West is essentially left-brained. The right brain is the seat of spirituality, creativity, spontaneity, emotion and intuition. The left brain is the seat of order, discipline, reason, structure and analysis. Both have their merits and demerits. The East is chaotic and disorderly, at least from the outside, but it has given rise to almost all the religions in the world. The West is orderly, disciplined and has given rise to science and the industrial revolution. But since science is based on separation, all its discoveries and inventions have only succeeded in destroying the world and its inhabitants. The West needs the East to understand the truths of life and how to live. The East needs the West to bring about more order and efficiency in their communities. But make no mistake about it. The East's role is the greater one – for it will show the way. Without that guidance, human society will go dreadfully wrong, as our present circumstances clearly reveal.

The final balance is the coming together of the head and heart. Both are needed, but the vital question remains the same as the one between the right and left brain. Who will call the shots? Without a doubt, the heart comes first. As Antoine de Saint-Exupery said in *The Little Prince*, "It is only with the heart that one can see rightly; what is essential is invisible to the eye."

The heart is like your compass which will always point you due north. If you follow your heart you will know what to do in any given situation. You will know who to trust and who not to. What decision you must take while at the crossroads. You will know what the right thing to do is each time you have to act. You will know what the next step in your path is. Almost everything will intuitively arise for you. The role of the head comes later. It will examine the decision we have arrived at and see if it holds water. Once the decision is taken, it will map the journey. It is the heart that tells us where to go, but it is the head that actually packs the bag, buys the ticket and boards the plane/train.

Most of us are head thinkers because our culture emphasises IQ (intellectual quotient) and simply ignores EQ (emotional quotient) and SQ (spiritual quotient). From a very young age, we are evaluated on the basis of our intelligence, not on how nice or wise we are, or how responsible. Standing first in class is really all that counts. But in the real world, the latter two are the qualities that pay off in the long run. How well you do at work is ultimately more a function of how much support you get from your colleagues than your brilliant brain.

More importantly, since our heart has the secrets to the truths of life, it is the heart that will guide us towards health, happiness, long-term success and harmony. The heart will prioritise marrying a good person rather than a good-looking or wealthy one. The heart will prioritise happiness over career progress and relationships over wealth, power or fame. The heart will cherish tiny gestures such as a little boy offering you a wildflower, a dog leaping at you with boundless joy or enjoying a packet of biscuits dipped in a cup of tea. The head, not knowing better, would rather have hothouse flowers, a show dog or tea in a five-star hotel.

We can cultivate our heart by becoming aware of our feelings and honouring them. Our feelings tell us exactly how we perceive every aspect of our lives. Attempting to push them aside and doing what is politically expedient or what favours self-interest will make us inauthentic and ultimately put us completely out of sync with life.

I have been a heart person almost all my life and it has held me in great stead. For starters, it has helped to carve out my own value system. I can be relied upon to side with humanitarian considerations rather than those that favour progress, technology or economic growth. I will, generally speaking, support the underdog rather than the top dog. I will always go running to the help of anyone who needs it. I will speak out against injustice.

My heart is my infallible counsel and I would be lost without it. And yet, I am a thinker, as well. I believe that I am a visionary and that I am able to foresee the future. Thus, perhaps, in this one area, I have got my balance right.

Do check out your own level of balance in all these areas and perhaps others, too. For we must reach the middle path in all things to qualify for enlightenment.

Lesson #29

Free Yourself from the Lure of Money

A very long time ago, I met a couple who had made money suddenly and dramatically when they opened a real estate agency in Pune. They had succeeded remarkably in their venture and soon became the city's leading realtors. I met them in Mumbai along with our mutual friend who had introduced us. They were holidaying in a plush beachside retreat close to my home. Amidst the conversation, I asked them what money meant to them. The husband responded by saying that it gave them freedom.

I responded that to me the greatest freedom was not needing money. I believed in it then, and I believe in it now.

At that time, I had just left my prestigious job as editor of *Society* magazine, and joined *Life Positive*. Not only was the salary considerably less than what I had been earning previously, but it also did not even have the perks that had been mine, such as a free house and a car. The situation became all the more financially fraught when, shortly after the move to *Life Positive*, I decided to invest in a flat, which consumed half of my salary. Tight though our budget was, my mother and I managed reasonably well.

Yes, those days were totally Spartan. I spent on nothing save the bare necessities. But that did not reduce my happiness in any way. We always had enough to eat and even to host family and friends. I had enough clothes from the past to get by and, occasionally, my family added to my wardrobe. One time I took out a whole lot of dupattas I was not using and reconstructed them as pretty kurtas.

But that was only the beginning. When I embarked on my austere lifestyle in 1996, it was an enforced move, for I simply starved my desires. In consequence, I became stingy with money and absolutely fearful about spending on even legitimate needs. I was terrified of looking at ads in newspapers and TV, lest I give in to their blandishment. How afraid I was of spending money even on towels and bedsheets or other necessary household items. Even today, one of my most fervent prayers of gratitude to God comes from the fact that I can now afford to buy pomegranates (which I need to soothe my stomach), as much as I want!

Now that I am finally making some money through my workshops, I am learning to free myself of my cramped and constricted approach and move into abundance. I strive to be at a place where I am not afraid of spending lakhs when needed, but not even a single rupee when not needed. At the same time, I never lose sight of the fact that my journey is to free myself of my desires and not stay stuck in them.

And even though I now buy a few more clothes than I actually need, I hope to reach a state when even that will be pruned.

Still, my lifestyle is essentially austere. I travel by buses and trains whenever possible. I do not buy jewellery, save a few silver trinkets. I do not use make-up at all, save for kajal and powder bindi. I rarely eat out, nor do I see too many movies in theatres. I do not cram my house with expensive bric-a-brac, for I prefer the beauty of handicrafts and folk art. My kitchen has just about enough for my needs for I am not at all interested in accumulating vessels.

I own only a one-bedroom apartment in Mumbai, and I am not interested in buying anything more. I don't own a vehicle, and I hope never to do so. When it comes to bags, shoes, watches and mobiles, I stay with just one, nor am I interested in shelling out for top-end products.

My one luxury would be travel, but as often as possible, I strive to hold a workshop in the places I go to, thereby actually earning from my travels. However, I sense that even my lust for travel is abating, and that I will be glad to stay rooted more and more at home. Yes, I spend a lot of money on gifts to family and friends, but that is a joy I do not want to deny myself. I also believe in giving to those in need, particularly those around me, and that, too, is something I hope to practice lifelong, and perhaps more and more.

I still have to heal myself of financial insecurity which keeps me focussed on making money. I do believe that once this drops, and it is already much less imperative than it once was, I will naturally adopt a much more thrifty life, because that is what I aspire for. Those who do not need money are the blessed of the land, for they are totally free of the world and its many traps. No need to suck up to the boss in order to feed the family. No need to take on jobs that militate against your ethics simply because the salary there is great.

When I was editor of *Life Positive* I met scores of people who would tell me that my job was their dream calling. Whenever I told them what I was earning, they would turn away disappointed, and say that they could not afford to sacrifice their salaries. This is undoubtedly very understandable when you have families. But too often, we sacrifice our dreams and our soul's calling in order to sustain a posh lifestyle.

I recall reading *The Autobiography of a Yogi* many years ago and being entranced by the life of Dandemis, a yogi of such renown that when Alexander the Great came to India, he asked to meet with him. Accordingly, an emissary was dispatched to find the yogi. He found him in a forest somewhere meditating and forthwith commanded him to get up and go to meet Alexander since that was his wish. Compliance would earn him rich rewards, but a refusal would be met with death.

Dandemis listened calmly to the order and told him that since he neither coveted gold nor feared death, he would not go to Alexander. Instead, if Alexander wanted to meet him, he should come to Dandemis. What absolute freedom to be able to refuse the imperial summons of a conqueror, because he was free of both craving and fear. Who can control such a man? He is absolutely free.

Lesson #30

Love Yourself

I firmly believe that one of the biggest reasons for me to have taken incarnation in this lifetime was to learn the secret of self-esteem, and perhaps also to teach it.

Ever since I can remember, I have had no concept of self-esteem whatsoever. As a child, any minor activity would trigger off a tornado of emotions. The boys in my class teasing me was nothing short of a catastrophe. A teacher scolding me was almost too much for me to bear. My mother often had to go to the school teacher and beg her to be gentler with me. Burdened with extreme sensitivity and no sense of self, it is a wonder that I emerged in one piece at all from my childhood.

My perilous sense of self-esteem showed up in a million ways. My sense of boundaries was so feeble that anyone could trample all over me and I would not (rather, could not) have raised a finger in protest. I remember playing on our lawn at 13 and receiving a gentle push from one of my friends, which was enough for me to topple over. A pushover, if ever there was one!

Because I had so little faith in my capabilities, I lived in a state of near panic, always fearful of what the next moment would bring, and absolutely terrified of taking on responsibilities. I remember attending a workshop called Forum in the early '80s (now called Landmark Forum) and when I was asked to introduce myself, I revealed forlornly,

"I'm no good." The absoluteness of that statement astonishes me today. But that was what I felt about myself then.

To be without self-esteem is like not having a skin. Even the slightest pressure can cause you to flinch. You see insults where none were intended, and you are forever defensive, always sure that you have goofed up and that everything is your fault. Because you have such a poor opinion of yourself, you are always looking for validation from outside yourself. This means that in your eagerness to please and win approval, you give away all your power.

Moreover, since your relationship with yourself is the foundation for how you live, love and work, an inability to love yourself affects everything in your life. Insecurity, fear, jealousy, envy, surge inside you and dictate your every action, because your lack of centre makes you very other-dependent. At the same time, your inability to love yourself makes it impossible to love anyone else, and all you are concerned with is that gaping hole within where love ought to be, making you desperate for love, which you keep looking for outside yourself.

While I was aware that I had a profound inferiority complex, I had little idea how to heal it. It was not until a year after my momentous awakening that I found the answers I was looking for. I was finding it more and more difficult to get into the no-ego space through my mantra ("It is other people's happiness that counts"). On inquiry, I could see that it was my poor self-esteem that was always pulling me down into reactivity, resistance and loops of negative thinking.

It was at that point that I decided that I was no longer going to force myself into focussing on others' happiness. It had to be a natural state. And I was going to find out how to do it. I guess that is when I became a seeker and stepped on the path. A momentous decision to be sure, but not knowing what a long journey it was going to be, I was insouciant enough to think it would be over in four short months.

My next step was to try and understand what self-esteem was and how I could attain it. The Universe is never too far away from a sincere seeker and, pretty soon, a friend manifested who was the embodiment of that state. Nothing perturbed him, he seemed to float in a vast sea of calm. Mistakes did not fluster him as they did me. He simply acknowledged them, and moved on. I was fascinated and studied him as much as I could.

In a few months' time, I got my reward. I was standing outside my sister's house in Colaba, waiting for my car to take me to a party that we were organising at *Society* magazine. I had been in a constant state of unhappiness ever since I had given up my mantra. For a moment though, I got distracted from the angst, and seemed to plumb into the depths of my being. Momentarily, I made contact with my Higher Self. I experienced it as a shining ball and, instinctively, realised that I was whole and perfect. There were no dents anywhere in me. The dents were all on the surface, but the real me was flawless.

It was a wondrous discovery, this distinction between the ego-personality and the Higher Self. It was a great relief to know that I was not fundamentally flawed. That all the flaws were on the surface, and could be healed.

To me, this is the foundation of perfect self-esteem. We are innately whole and perfect. Everything else is conditioning. Therefore, there is no question of building up self-esteem. We do not need to attempt to stack it up through achievements, fame, fortune or power. None of these can heal us, because we do not need to heal. We simply have to eliminate the conditioning. For anyone wanting to work on themselves, this is such a reassuring realisation. I had, after all, been brought up on Sigmund Freud, who seemed to discover more and more darkness the deeper he went into the unconscious. How wonderful to know then that the end of the journey would bring us to our real self, and that happiness, perfection, peace and love were who we really were.

In time, I made my acquaintance with the Upanishads and Vedanta, and that enlarged the picture for me while reinforcing my insight. I discovered that the core of Vedantic thought is the recognition that the Creator and the created were One and that, in effect, we were both Divine and connected. We were part of the Creator. We were Godstuff. How then, could we not be whole and perfect?

Bolstered with this understanding, I decided to instil this insight within myself, for to my surprise, the realisation did not in any way change my self-esteem.

In a beautiful way, the Universe conspires to bring to us what we need in order to move to the next step, I came across an article that talked about the powers of the subconscious mind. I learnt that if we wanted to change ourselves at the deepest level, we needed to change the subconscious mind. The article explained that the best way to do that was to go to the Alpha state and then affirm the statements we wanted to make. We were to use the present tense and frame our affirmation positively. My mind was too chaotic for me to move easily into the Alpha stage, but I made up for it by repeating my phrase "I am whole and perfect" ad infinitum. Slowly, something seemed to be moving and changing in my heart region.

About four months later, I felt as if a plate had come and covered a pit that I was wont to fall into, each time I got into a depression. I understood this development to mean that I would no longer plunge into a depression, which meant that I was now free to really look at myself and heal myself of my conditioning without the fear that it would send me skydiving into lunacy. Later, someone explained to me that my heart chakra had opened at that stage.

Sixteen years of depression had done terrible things to my psyche. I had let myself go completely and steeped myself in indifference and inertia. My memory was shot to bits. My sense of focus and concentration had dissipated. I had no capacity for organisation, efficiency and discipline. My will power and self-control were both nil. Had I not worked on my self-esteem before I confronted myself, I would not have been able to take the shock – I would surely have gone through a nervous breakdown. As it is, it was terrible to witness what had become of my mind, and it took me years and years of constant awareness and acceptance of it to even begin healing it.

So while the insight had given me a basic level of self-esteem, I was nowhere near healing myself of the huge quantities of conditioning that stood between me and my whole and perfect self. It has been 29 years since I first embarked on the path. I am sorry to say I still have some way to go before I can fully experience perfect self-esteem.

But the years have not been in vain. Instead of having no self-esteem, I have a reasonable amount of it, though my boundaries are still not perfect and I am still not able to protect myself perfectly from those who violate my space. I still have vestiges of insecurity that make me cranky and uptight at times.

Nevertheless, every day I am changing for the better. My confidence and capabilities are building up, love and joy surge within me most of the time, and a calm and a presence that I have never before enjoyed is pervading me. The panic, anxiety, worry and fear in which I used to be marinated are gradually dissipating. It is wondrous. The centre that was always missing is gradually forming. You need to be as fragmented as I was to appreciate what anything approaching wholeness feels like.

My own inner excavation convinces me that self-esteem is the vital key to an effective, happy and harmonious life. Nothing will work for us unless our self-esteem is perfect. So, cultivate it if you find it less than perfect.

My understanding of self-esteem has been greatly enhanced by my study of Nathaniel Branden's book, *The Six Pillars of Self-Esteem.* He made me understand that self-esteem has two components to it. One is self-efficacy or the knowing that you are capable of coping with the challenges of life. The other is self-worth, which enables you to recognise that you deserve the very best that life can offer you. That you are whole within.

When these two components are in place, your life will naturally bloom. You will find yourself aligned to life instead of opposed to it. Instead of sabotaging every opportunity for success, love, happiness or other precious gifts, you will start to back yourself, believe in yourself, forgive yourself when you goof up and reaffirm yourself to your goals.

With self-esteem, life turns the right side up.

Lesson #31

Women Will Show the Way

It is March 8th, 2019, as I write this. An apt moment indeed to reflect on my views on womankind and what being a woman means to me.

I do not remember having any fixed ideas about being a woman growing up. I was not a feminist. I was not drawn to the movement's aggressive anti-male stance, even though I had a couple of ardent feminist friends. At the same time, I was not at all aware of the innate strengths of a woman (perhaps because I had not yet tapped them from within myself). Nor do I remember being someone who thought that the male sex was superior, because I never yearned to be a boy or strove to be as good as a man. My view on the genders was simply dormant.

The shift happened after the awakening. I was looking at life the right side up and many things became very clear to me. It was evident that what passed for strength in our society was nothing but oppression and controlism. Anyone who could control or command another person was considered to be strong and admirable. I recognised that men had a greater capacity to do this, perhaps because of their superior physical strength as well as their economic advantage, and that this was generally considered to be admirable.

My spiritual experience had taught me that real strength was the capacity to expand oneself to accept another, and that binding another to one's will was an act of violence that ought not to be condoned. It completely changed the way I viewed the male-female relationship. Men commanded and women obeyed, but was this equation in the interests of either gender? Men subsequently grew up with a sense of entitlement based on feeling superior to women, while women grew up feeling powerless with an inability to stand up for themselves or direct their own life choices. Considering that we are here on Planet Earth to grow to the highest version of ourselves and that we are all equally bestowed with freedom of will, this skewed equation clearly seemed to be a creation of the male sex rather than an act of God. Above all, both men and women, or indeed every particle of existence, was part of God and, therefore, equally sacred. In what way then could one sex rule over another?

It was around then that I made acquaintance with the word 'patriarchy' of which one of the dictionary definitions is 'a system of society or government where men hold the power and women are largely excluded from it'. Looking around society, at the life of my family members and friends, and finally at my own life, it became shockingly clear how patriarchal Indian society was. Indeed, we live in a patriarchal age, and women all over the world are making Herculean efforts to claim their power, but Indian society is even more sunk in it. Having been born into a household of only girls, and having worked generally in female-dominated small media houses, I personally did not have too much exposure to patriarchy, but the fact that my sisters and I owe our existence to my parents' ceaseless strife for a boy was not lost on me. Further, it was impossible not to miss society's general sentiment that women were a burden and needed to be protected, looked after, told what to do and, more often than not, controlled. In time, like most women I knew, it became part of my mission in life to help uplift women and support them to reclaim their power.

I asked myself on what was the patriarchal claim to superiority based? On their physical strength? Their aptitude for numbers and mechanics? Their mastery in the world of work? But were these the most important things in life?

I looked at women's work – neglected and despised for aeons. Cooking food, taking care of the young and the old, maintaining relationships and bonds, running and creating a home. Women take care of life. And what could possibly be more important than that? This was a genuine revelation to me. Really, what could be more important than taking care of life?

I looked deeper and found the qualities that made them adept at this. Softness, gentleness, nurturance, conciliation, co-operation, resilience, compassion and love. To me, these qualities seemed glorious. They were what the world was so desperately in need of.

The world did not need despots and dictators, or venal politicians whose only aim was to fill their coffers. The world did not need advertising or marketing geniuses adept at creating needs in people that they had previously not had. The world did not need conquerors and kings who went about raping and destroying the world. The world needed healers, menders and artists. It needed people who would bring together, not split apart. It needed those who would nurture, not destroy. It needed all the compassion and love it could use, that women have long been practised in giving.

At the heart of patriarchy, I suspect, is a deep resentment of a woman's real strength, which is her ability to give birth to and nurture life; side by side, the patriarchy nursed an equally deep commitment to keep her from recognising the importance of that. Therefore, it was necessary to make birthing and nurturing life seem trivial, though you cannot go through life for too long without recognising the supreme importance of this task, for our very survival hinges on it. If love, sacrifice and acceptance were not at the heart of the family, and if the woman were not the heart of the family, I truly doubt if civilisation would have even continued. It would have collapsed in a welter of violence, competition, control and self-destruction.

Fortunately, if there is one success story that post-independent India can be proud of, it is the rate at which women have progressed. Being underdogs gave them the endurance and resilience they needed to pull themselves up. Slowly, without letting go of their responsibilities towards home and family, women have found their place in the world. Once derided for their poor intellect, they are now proving their worth in every arena. It is now almost commonplace to have girls score higher over boys in school- and college-level examinations.

Interestingly, some of the most crucial jobs in society were given over to women simply because they were too low-paying to interest men. Teaching is a powerful way to influence future generations, and it has been almost fully dominated by women, at least, when it comes to schools. Media, especially the magazine and the book publishing worlds, is another sector where women dominate and this, too, is a highly influential zone. I know of no study that has actually mapped the impact of this trend, but perhaps it has caused our society to become a little more balanced when it comes to the gender equation.

The whole world will benefit when women learn to develop a healthy appreciation for who they are and begin to value themselves. When they stop toeing the line set by society, when they start making their own decisions about education, work, marriage and having children, when they develop the self-confidence and self-assurance to embrace and nurture their talents and gifts, when they refuse to be put down or made less of, not only will the children they bring up imbibe these values, but they will be able to contribute creatively towards making the world a better place.

Many gurus have reiterated and I, for one, wholeheartedly believe that the Spiritual Age will only emerge through women. Spiritual teacher and author of *The Power of Now*, Eckhart Tolle, said it best in that same book. He says: "Generally speaking, it is easier for a woman to feel and be in her body, so she is naturally closer to Being, and potentially closer to enlightenment than a man."

He also states that "the energy frequency of the mind appears to be essentially male. The mind resists, fights for control, uses, manipulates . . ."

He continues: "To go beyond the mind and reconnect with the deeper reality of Being, very different qualities are needed: surrender, non-judgement, an openness that allows life to be instead of resisting it, the capacity to hold all things in the loving embrace of your knowing. All these qualities are much more closely related to the female principle."

Only if we women take ourselves seriously, appreciate our innate strengths and heal ourselves of the many wounds dealt by centuries of patriarchy, will the world heal and become whole.

What are the areas women need to heal?

First and foremost is self-esteem. The consequence of centuries of oppression is fractured self-esteem in the vast majority of the female population. Our boundaries are weak, we are incorrigible people pleasers, we do not speak up for ourselves, we allow ourselves to be taken for granted and we are in perpetual doubt about our capabilities.

Secondly, we need to heal ourselves of our excessive emotionalism. I believe that our emotions are a profound strength but because of poor self-esteem, they can often make us reactive, cranky, moody and cause us to make poor decisions. In order to achieve sound emotional intelligence, we must attain control over our emotions. The self-esteem journey will help us enormously in this area. In addition, I would urge women to become aware of their emotions and strive to accept them. Pushing them away will strengthen them. Peacefully accepting them will enable them to heal and dissipate.

We also need to strengthen the masculine within us, just as men need to strengthen their feminine side. We need to increase our dynamism, ease with numbers and other such masculine strengths.

So, my dear sisters. Awake, arise and go forth. The world needs us. The next step is in our hands.

Lesson #32

Never Try to Convert Others

I call it the Born Again Syndrome. The urge to run and tell others as soon as you get a glimmer of light or insight, and insist that they have to believe or practise likewise.

Well, been there, done that, and I am here to tell you that it never works! Spiritual truths can only be received by a receptive mind. And the moment we foist our truths upon others, we alienate them. No one wants to be told what to think or who to believe in. The last thing they want is someone filled with a missionary zeal to pursue them grimly. The more you run after them, the more they take to their heels.

I was once a part of what was then called Forum (now called Landmark Forum). Their marketing policy was simple. They did not have one. Instead, all past participants were required to tell others about their programme and persuade them to come for an introductory class.

After a year of imparting the spiel about the course, I quit before people actually turned tail and fled.

Of course, when the Universe bestowed me with my spiritual awakening, my Forum experience did not dampen the ardour with which I went around trying to get people to focus on other people's happiness and not their own. Most looked at me with puzzled uncomprehending eyes. I was most concerned about my own family, particularly one sister who was going through a hard time. Try as I would, I could not get through and, finally, the penny dropped.

As much as I feared that my sister would plunge into misery if I did not immediately rescue her with my mantra of focussing on the other's happiness, I had to let her be. Everyone had their own time for awakening and my wanting to hasten hers only came in the way.

One of the things that had most struck me after my Awakening was that the truth had been all over the place. Many books that I had read had been luminous with the wisdom of prioritising another's happiness. The Bible was chock-full of it. What was Christ's injunction to love one's neighbour as oneself, but a version of my own insight to prioritise the happiness of the other? And yet, I had not understood any of it because I was spiritually blind. I recognised that the Truth could stand in front of me emblazoned on a 10-foot tall board, but I would still not see it unless I was ready.

With that, fortunately, my feeble attempts at proselytisation fell away and I was finally able to let others be.

That, of course, did not mean that I would not share my precious experiences and insights with others. I had benefitted from the wisdom of others and I knew that I was meant to pass on my own. I could see that all of us were walking the same path; some ahead of us, who would pass on the torch of their own understanding, and some behind us, to whom we were obliged to pass on our truths.

At the same time, my Christian background had taught me that ascending a pulpit and thundering to the laity was a sure turn-off. I could not remember the number of sermons I had recoiled from, mentally questioning the speaker's right to tell others to repent and not sin.

I resorted instead to sharing my thoughts and experiences from a platform of equality. I was a seeker, just like the other, and I did not need to pretend to know it all or have it all. I did not have to pretend to be enlightened in order to impact my fellow travellers.

I also knew that intimacy only came through equality. The moment one assumed the stance of superiority or inferiority, intimacy was lost.

These ideas influenced my writing style. As an editor, it also influenced the kind of articles I preferred to publish in *Life Positive*. I steered clear of 'gyan', knowledge-intensive pieces that came from a space of knowing it all. I preferred, instead, to use articles where the author shared their own experiences and insights and left it to the reader to pick up whatever they wished.

I found that this was a much more effective and softer way of imparting one's truths. There was no proselytisation, there was mere sharing. To me, it is quite clear that there is nothing more compelling than a story, and when we share our stories without attempting any ascendency over the other, we give them the space they need. Other people's stories inspire and convince us in a way 'gyan' cannot, that we, too, can change. Many *Life Positive* readers appreciated this approach and sent us letters comparing the magazine to a mother giving her children *sanskars*.

So, yes, I did spread the word, but I left the other with the freedom to choose or reject it. And that I have found, is the best way to get through to the other.

Lesson #33

Never Accept Bad Behaviour

As one who has suffered from extremely poor self-esteem most of her life, it took me a very long time to learn to say no to bad behaviour. I am probably still not the best at it, for true mastery is to respond firmly but politely while I might still have an edge in my voice.

Nevertheless, I certainly have progressed from the time when I would be so thrown by what others said or did and at the same time so devoid of inner strength that, more often than not, I would simply say nothing or, even worse, kowtow to their disrespectful demands!

My ongoing inner work came to my rescue here and, slowly, my sense of self became stronger. I began to develop the self-respect and assertiveness needed to draw boundaries and prevent people from taking advantage of me, taking me for granted, running me down, making fun of me, blaming me for what was not my fault or any of the scores of poor behaviour with which we humans try and get power over another.

Even though this is a generalisation, I cannot help but observe that most women (of course, many men as well) are unable to defend themselves when put down or ridiculed. One of the reasons is surely the centuries of patriarchal control we were subject to. Most of us are people pleasers (another manifestation of poor self-esteem) and saying something that may displease or annoy another gives us great anxiety.

Nevertheless, man or woman, not putting up with bad behaviour is an essential part of one's journey to becoming a self-respecting, dignified human being.

So, what exactly is bad behaviour? We all know it when we face it. These are the moments we feel disrespected or used. It could be going to meet a friend after giving them prior notice and finding him or her too busy to spend time with you. It could be someone who never picks up your calls or returns them. It could be someone who promises to call you and fails to do so repeatedly. It could be a colleague who contrives to make you do their work, without your quite knowing how. It could be someone stealing your work and passing it off as their own. Or sharing your posts on Facebook without attributing it to you. It could be someone who talks to you when they feel like it and ignores you at other times. It could be snide remarks or cruel ridicule meant to put you down. It could be slurs against your caste, community, colour and sex. It could be flagrant putdowns from persons of authority such as the boss or one's parents or one's spouse.

The world will pull you down if you let it. People will treat you exactly as you think you deserve to be treated. Thus, if you cannot rise to your own defence when insulted or dominated, everyone will ride roughshod over you. If you cannot establish sound boundaries between you and the other, you will find that everyone will breach the boundaries and walk all over you.

Thus, since the problem stems from your own relationship with yourself, that is where you need to start. We need to build up our self-esteem. Most of us are unaware that we think poorly of ourselves. We are under-confident of our capacity to handle life's challenges and we really don't think we are worth much. Self-worth is an indication of how valuable we think we are. People with healthy self-esteem have a good opinion of themselves. They will not permit disrespectful behaviour towards themselves. They will not permit others to control or command them. The reins of their lives are held quite firmly in their own hands.

This is what we need to aspire to. Learning to love ourselves is a long and difficult task (as I know from experience) but it can be done. And once we accomplish that, everything else will resolve itself. Our self-esteem will give out the clear message that we are not to be messed with, and people will watch their step with you.

The less we put up with bad behaviour, the less bad behaviour we will be subject to. People back off from those they perceive as strong enough to take them on and direct their crude comments at the unsure and the under-confident. Eventually, there will be less bad behaviour on the whole on the planet, once we all learn to stand up for ourselves.

But there is another very important reason why we need to say no to bad behaviour and that is because it is not in the best interest of the perpetrator to practice such behaviour. Not only is the person storing up bad karma, but he or she is also not being his best version. When you compassionately correct someone because it is not in their best interest to behave badly, what you say and how you say it will be markedly different. And you may actually be able to be a transformative agent in their lives.

Lesson #34
Satyamev Jayate
(Truth Alone Triumphs)

This profound saying, which also happens to be India's national motto, does not yield its meaning at first glance. Does only the truth triumph? This is a question that consumes all those of us who have writhed at the way falsehood seems to be flourishing everywhere. But the longer you live, the more things that once seemed muddled begin to clarify. You realise that what works in the short-term may not work in the long-term. Get-rich-quick tactics are employed by those too unscrupulous to care about their long-term reputation. Those who value their reputation will never squander them in pursuit of easy money. Many amoral or foolish practices make sense in the short run, but will reveal their futility in the fullness of time.

In the long-term, the truth alone triumphs in a million different ways. Take the field of art and literature. Pretender after pretender will make a brief splash on centre stage, and will disappear just as quickly unless his claim to fame is backed solidly on merit. History will only remember the artist whose work is based on truth.

I remember a little limerick that I read in my 20s. This is how it went:

There is this wonderful family called Stein,
There's Gert, and there's Ep, and there's Ein,
Gert's poems are bunk, Ep's statues are junk,
And no one can understand Ein.

The writer was referring to a poet called Gertrude Stein and a sculptor called Epstein, both of whom have mercifully been relegated to history's dustbin. Einstein is still relevant and that is because his discoveries were the truth.

Similarly, all systems, perspectives and points of view unaligned to Oneness (which is the fundamental truth of life) will dissolve and disappear in time. We are already seeing this happen during our present times. About 300 years ago or so, French philosopher Rene Descartes, and a few other leading intellectuals of the time, came forward with the theory that only what could be verified by the senses was reliable and should be taken for the truth. All the rest was subjective and not to be included. "I think therefore I am" was the credo of this new understanding that validated only the material plane. All things of the soul and spirit were banished because they were not objective. Thus, the existence of a table or a chair was admitted as the truth, but not the existence of God or the soul.

This was the plank on which modern civilisation is built and its underlying premise is fragmentation and separation. The Universe is deemed a random celestial accident; there is no innate meaning to life, nor any coherence to the life experience. We come into being and get out of it without volition or meaning. All of life is just a random event and there is no connection between any of it.

Thus, if you see, modern medicine does not regard the body, mind and spirit as connected, modern architecture does not see a larger connection with the direction of the winds or the position of the stars, and modern agriculture insouciantly introduces poison into our food through chemical fertilizers and pesticides without ever fearing that it would affect us, because where is the connection? All modern systems are premised on separation and fragmentation.

Today, however, this understanding is itself fragmenting into a million shards as Satya or Truth begins its majestic appearance across the landscape of our times. We are increasingly recognising the shortfalls of modern medicine, which only fixes symptoms and never looks for the underlying cause, usually to be found in the mind or spirit. Moreover, its approach is essentially violent, focussing on killing the viruses and germs, unlike traditional therapies which focus on building up immunity and not destroying germs.

Similarly, modern architecture is challenged by traditional modalities like Feng Shui and Vastu Shastra which operate on the basis of a profound connection between the micro and the macro, and also by recognising that an intelligent harnessing of this connection will positively impact the happiness and health of inhabitants of buildings. Traditional wisdom, which architecture borrows from, recognised that the Universe is made of energy and that the infusion of positive energy into our houses can only happen through alignment with the larger whole.

Fragmented thinking created the folly that is modern farming. Today, there is enough and more evidence that all the poison unthinkingly drizzled upon plants and soil have seeped their way into everything we eat, killing innumerable species in the bargain (including sparrows and earthworms), and creating grave diseases for mankind. Such is the danger of fragmented thinking.

Likewise, modern education, whose focus is solely on earning a livelihood and which ignores vital aspects such as character building or developing emotional intelligence, is increasingly churning out students unable to cope with the realities of life even at the workplace, although they have trained for that very thing for decades. The concept of benefitting the whole person so that he can serve the whole society is missing in this narrow conception of life as merely a livelihood.

This fragmented understanding has influenced what passes as modern economy, where profit is given the highest priority and all of life is harnessed in achieving this goal. Thus nature becomes a resource and human beings labour. Because of the indifference to the larger whole, the single-minded focus on the economy has destroyed and damaged the environment beyond belief, fed mankind's greed for more and more and created an atmosphere of war and violence.

The whole explosion of conflict at the individual and collective level is once again based on the opportunistic principle that one must only look out for oneself, since there is no innate connection with the other. Thus, today, man is at unrest with himself as he looks for happiness through possessions, the family is splintering and squabbling as the virus of more and more grows rapidly, and at the societal level, unrest, sexual abuse and scarcity are creating unprecedented turmoil in our lives.

History has often stood testimony to the rise and fall of empires and nations. The Greek Empire had its moment in the sun and then sank into oblivion. So, too, the Roman Empire. In recent times, the mighty British Empire, whose boast was that the sun never set upon it, has found itself completely eclipsed. Only the Indian and Chinese civilisations, despite their antiquity (and invasion of communism in the case of the Chinese) can be said to be still alive, and it is important that we ask ourselves why.

Could it be that they were founded on true principles – on a holistic understanding of life? I can certainly testify that the Indian civilisation is based on the truth of Oneness and all its ancient systems revolved on this fulcrum. Self-realisation was considered to be the end game of the process of living, a purpose served by all its systems be it education, language, medicine or architecture. Therefore, despite the invasion of the Mughals and the British, the culture absorbed, accepted and remained its essential self. Being founded on true principles, it was saved from extinction.

These examples apart, we will find that in our own lives, truth triumphs time and again. How many times have our lies been found out? How many times have the illusions we nursed about ourselves and others been shattered? How many times have we betrayed and been betrayed, and the truth revealed itself? Life tends to nose these things out because it inexorably tends towards the truth. Look at the way the murder of Sheena Bora came out three years after she went missing. Those who murdered her probably had been quite confident that they got away with it, but the long arm of the truth nabbed them eventually.

Indeed, our progress towards self-realisation will really depend on how ready we are to see through the illusions with which Maya has woven her deceptive net, and to align ourselves with the truth. What are these illusions? One of them, as Yudhisthir astutely observed, is that we see death all around us, but never think that we, too, are going to die. Another is our belief that being in the past and the future are valid states, when, in actuality, the past is gone and nothing can change it, and the unborn future only exists in our imagination. Another illusion is that we are the ego-self with its attributes of thought and emotions, when our true nature is Godhead. Slowly and irrevocably, life will move us gradually towards penetrating these illusions and attaining the truth of life, which alone is enlightenment.

Lesson #35

Every Weakness Has Its Strength, and Every Strength Its Weakness

Life is paradoxical and, therefore, hard to penetrate. It is only through trial and error that we begin to understand the secrets it contains within itself.

One of these many secrets is the two-sidedness of any quality that we may possess. What may appear to be a strength that we are legitimately proud of, may turn out to host a covert little weakness. That is not all. The weakness that we are ashamed of and have been resisting for years, may turn out to have a strength hidden on the underside.

For instance, I am guilty of having a poor hold on facts and, for the life of me, can never get dates, places and names right. They don't register in my vague, dreamy world. I still remember having spent an inglorious four months in my youth at a tabloid called *Blitz*, which was unabashedly sensationalistic. The journalists were forever emerging with one exposé after another. I lived in daily fear that my fact phobia would earn me a lawsuit from some irate party or other.

Since journalism was all about mastery over facts, I used to consider myself a poor journalist. It was only after my awakening that I realised that yes, I would probably be a terrible investigative reporter, but my breadth of perspective, depth of clarity and big-picture thinking made me a good thinker and, indeed, a visionary. I was someone who may not be very good on the field gathering data, but I was excellent at putting the data together and figuring out what it meant. I was also excellent at envisaging the way ahead, not just for society as a whole but also for the organisation I worked with. So, yes, I may not have made a good soldier, but I was a pretty good general.

Similarly, growing up, I was deeply ashamed of my lack of practical acumen and housewifely capabilities. It also made me the object of other people's judgements when I let the milk boil over, the vegetable burn, forgot to note the *dhobi's* account, overshot my station while commuting by train or even forgot to pay my bills. Although inner work has made me far better in this zone, I am still a far cry from the organised efficient homemakers that I see around me. However, the upside of this unfortunate shortcoming is that my cloud of abstraction is really caused by an active imagination and a capacity to ponder over things. I have about 10 commentaries running in my mind at any given time. Most of it is just idle thinking, but some of it comes out of my imagination being gripped by an idea or a thought. So, yes, I may be a sloppy housewife but thanks to that, I am an excellent writer.

Similarly, I am hopeless at observing things right in front of my eyes. I rarely notice the details of the cut and style or colour of what people are wearing (unless it really seizes my fancy), or their jewellery, and whether their shoes match their clothes. I can wander around a neighbourhood locked in a brown study, completely oblivious of all that I see. So, my sensory quotient is admittedly poor but my psychic quotient is high. I am very perceptive about people's emotional and psychological states and can read deep into their nature and character. When I enter a room, I can figure out whether there is harmony among its occupants or whether there is some kind of tension among them. My low sensory intelligence is, no doubt, caused by my high intuition. According to the Myers Briggs Type Indicator (MBTI), people draw their information from two things – either through their senses or through their intuitive knowing. Since I adore being intuitive, I am willing to compromise on the limited information provided by my senses, even though it embroils me in innumerable practical difficulties.

Similarly, society today places a great premium on efficiency, sense of organisation and a capacity to plan their lives. As you may have guessed by now, I certainly cannot claim to have these sterling qualities as part of my mental make-up. But have you noticed that all this can come in the way of spontaneity and a capacity to seize the moment? I do claim to be spontaneous. Even though sometimes that spills over into impulsivity, my spirit is essentially natural and spontaneous and am happy to seize the fun in the moment and go for a spur-of-the-minute drive or a movie, without worrying about whether that would torpedo my carefully planned day.

Being emotional is often considered to be a weakness by those who pride themselves on being rational and calm. It is true that highly emotional people tend to have their emotions on overdrive very often and foam in the mouth once in a while, but look at what comes with it! Their capacity to feel deeply can give them moments of bliss throughout the day, triggered by the slightest of things such as when they see kittens or puppies playing, flowering trees splashing the horizon with colour, a mother cuddling her child, a toddler's smile, children playing or seeing the moon float above, calm and bright.

Besides, our capacity to feel is a reflection of our capacity to experience life. The calm, cool rational ones will never know the ecstasy emotional people are capable of, nor will they be able to invest themselves into life as much as emotional people can, for their capacity to care is powerful.

Moreover, being emotional helps you develop empathy and sympathy with the suffering of others. Most of all, no artist can be great if he or she cannot feel, for the work grows in life to the exact proportion that one is able to feel. Therefore, since being emotional has a wealth of advantages that the rational thinker cannot even conceive of, give thanks for the invaluable capacity to feel that enables life to be so much more multi-dimensional than it may appear to the overly rational. The present crisis of modern life is caused by an excess of head thinking and not enough heartfulness. So, those of us who can still feel should really be grateful that we are setting right this balance.

And, so it goes with so many other qualities. Just keep looking at all the gifts your weaknesses hold. You will be amazed.

Of course, this does not mean we should not strive to correct our imbalances. We definitely should. Our road to enlightenment has to include arriving at a balance in all or most aspects of our lives. At the same time, we need to recognise that what society has traditionally put down may actually have some surprising strengths that perhaps the world is presently in need of.

Lesson #36

Advantage Underdogs

For a few centuries, we Indians were underdogs when it came to having a global status. Having been conquered and enslaved, first by the Mughals and then by the British, our national self-esteem was shattered, and faith in our native philosophy destroyed. We, therefore, entered independence with no more self-determination than a small baby and simply bought the Western worldview hook, line and sinker.

It has taken us all these many years to achieve some modicum of discrimination with which to review their culture and see what will work for us and what will not. To recognise that we are a different people with a different climate, geography and culture, and therefore our needs are very different from theirs is still a hard struggle for us. In this area, we are still a work in progress, but I long for the time when we will actually own our unique philosophy and perspective of life and live in accordance with that.

At the same time, what I really want to emphasise here are the benefits that we gained during our underdog era. For one thing, since the West did not care for our perspectives, art or culture, we had to learn theirs in order to belong. The British had left us knowledge of the English language and therefore we had access to their cultures. Thus, we became avid consumers of their books, art, music, food, technology and so much else. But since ours is a living civilisation, we also have access to our own cultural, artistic, spiritual and culinary heritage. I believe that this gives us an invaluable edge over other cultures, for we have so much richer a palimpsest of influences. I am confident that as soon as our self-esteem becomes healthy, we will see an explosion of creative and spiritual genius emerging from this land.

Secondly, our knowledge of the English language has not only enabled us to emerge with world-class literature but has given us a fabulous advantage in the ongoing Western civilisation.

Thirdly, we are so much more familiar with their way of life than they are with ours. Their geography, history and mythologies are as familiar to us as our own. Thus our general knowledge is certainly better than theirs.

Fourthly, as underdogs, we had to work for acceptance, for jobs in their countries and for recognition. Perforce, we had to work hard. All that has given us a great deal of success in these alien lands. In the US, for instance, Indians are the richest community of immigrants, considering that many of them are either doctors or IT professionals.

Such advantages are the lot of anyone or any section of people who have been put down and oppressed for a long period of time. Normally, we tend to regard such people with empathy and sympathy, but rarely do we consider that these very circumstances may be their secret strength.

Here in India, I am constantly amazed at the resilience, acceptance and strength of the economically underprivileged. Even though they may have to contend with the constant struggle for money as well as a host of difficulties that living on the edge entails, the maids I have had have never lost their smiles for more than a couple of days. They seem to straddle with ease problems that would have decimated the rest of us. One of my maids lost her granddaughter to illness, her son-in-law to suicide and her husband to cancer. And yet, there was Gauri, always dignified and graceful, looking after me and my house with love and devotion.

It is their hard life that has given them such an

adamantine strength. Walking barefoot on the earth gives them the grounding that the rest of us have no access to. Facing impossible situations day in and day out forces them to focus on the moment alone, for they would otherwise topple into madness.

Lack of money forces them to walk when others would take a bus, train, cab or private car, to endure illnesses without taking medicines, to eat the simplest food, which, thanks to the fact that they do not have a refrigerator, is always freshly cooked. All this invests them with physical and mental health and strength.

Their difficult circumstance also gives them access to the truths of life. The poor know what the richer allow themselves to forget – that money is not a priority in leading a good life. Relationships, integrity and selflessness are of far more value. I had a maid who would always return from her occasional trips to her native Tamil Nadu with rice and coconuts which she would share with us. When I asked her why she was giving us when we could afford to buy our own rice, she said it gave her joy to share!

Perhaps the greatest success story of any community that has used its underdog status to rise dramatically to success, freedom and capability is the woman's story.

Although women have been suppressed for millennia all over the world, look how amazingly we have crafted liberation for ourselves. Traditionally forced to stay at home and allow their talents to rust, modern women not only continue to field the home front by taking on the lion's share of household responsibilities such as cooking, taking care of children, running the house and a million other domestic duties, but they have also forged out into the outside world and have taken on the jobs that were once decreed to be the exclusive territory of men. With few exceptions, women excel in all areas and, although it is still a man's world, every day women are expanding their reach.

Economic independence is the game changer that has empowered them to free themselves of the clutches of husbands, fathers and brothers, and take their lives forward. Today, more and more women are recognising that they do not need marriage, especially when the odds are stacked so cruelly against them in India. Why marry, when your parents have to give a hefty dowry to the boy's family, even though you are earning as much as he is? Why marry, when you are expected to fit meekly into the many roles expected of you in the joint family, and essentially be an unpaid servant in the house? Why marry when you will have to bear most of the burden of running the house and invariably compromise on your career so that your husband can smoothly rise up the ladder?

Unless Indian society rewrites these rules, and unless men are willing to become partners in marriage instead of being the boss, women may choose to lead independent lives and men may be forced to look after themselves.

After centuries of ruling over the women in their lives, it is hard for men to give up their power. But the force of evolution will compel them to. Women have gone ahead, and men have no choice but to follow.

These are just a few examples but they dramatically illustrate the spiritual principle that runs through life. Comforts, conveniences and privileges may not really be the blessings we think they are. If incarnation on Planet Earth is for the purpose of growing as human beings, then the hard life of physical work and endurance better equips us for it. The sages have always maintained that what does not kill us makes us stronger. So, evaluate the areas in your life where you are the underdog and optimise the hidden strength it holds. At the same time, evaluate the many areas of your life where you may be the top dog, and see how this status may have added to your complacence, need for power and will to exploit and, vigilantly, root out these tendencies.

Lesson #37

True Invulnerability Comes from Vulnerability

I remember the time I and five of my friends went out for a weekend break. Most of us were seekers and had worked on ourselves. One night, the six of us stayed up and shared our life histories with each other. The seekers among us were unabashedly open. We talked about our love affairs, our moments in the sun and in the shade, but one lady stayed mum. We never got to know the real part of her, the pains she had endured or her struggles to become herself. She remained an enigma to us, perhaps because she was still an enigma to herself. This beautiful talented woman had not fully confronted herself and, therefore, was unable to share the depth of her being with us.

My mother's life, on the other hand, was an open book. Anyone was free to read any line, page or chapter. I recall a friend of mine quite amazed at my mother's candour as she shared some of the challenges she had met and confronted, including financial privation. I explained to him that she saw no reason to be ashamed of anything in her life.

My friend could not believe it was possible to be so open about oneself.

I remember the time when I kept myself completely under wraps because I was so heartily ashamed of the person I was. I dare not open up to anyone lest they reject me, and friendships never ever reached the zone of intimacy. As I say, moving into the spiritual zone and bringing up to consciousness all the rejected parts of me brought about a revolution, but the turning point was the moment I decided to face my conditioning. To my horror, I discovered what a mess I had made of my mind in the intervening years between my depression 16 years ago to the time of my awakening. My focus was zero, my memory was zero, my discipline was zero, my self-control was zero. I cringed at my ravaged self, but even so, I was told by my inner voice that the only way to heal was to talk about it. Accordingly, despite wanting to shroud my disabilities with the deepest darkness, I felt compelled to share about it in my *Life Positive* columns. Oddly enough, the more I bared my glaring weaknesses, the less they troubled me, and the more I accepted them. I also began to heal from them. Thus began my journey into vulnerability and with every day, I gather fresh courage to open my heart and my soul to those around me.

My goal is to lead a totally transparent life, unafraid to own anything about my past or present. This does not mean I will make an open present of my life to anyone at all. If the motive of the other is to pry or put me down, I choose to be reticent, but when the other is coming from a good space I am very happy to share myself as openly and honestly as I can.

As a writer, too, I choose to be vulnerable. To share the truths of myself and my life as faithfully as I can. Sometimes, I will hesitate to divulge a piece of information that I feel may expose me to judgement even more than usual. But that is exactly what I compel myself to share. Were I to give in to the fear of judgement, I would cease to be vulnerable, for this is the very thing that stops most of us from opening up. In the process, we end up giving too much power to public opinion or to the other, and thereby disempower ourselves. Inevitably, it is this very piece of information that

I contemplated withholding that readers often acknowledge or appreciate, sharing that it had helped them to accept the very same thing within them.

When you dismantle your armour, you allow others to do so, too.

Living vulnerably means to permit yourself to feel what you feel, and think what you think. It also means being willing to share these feelings and thoughts with others. For instance, if you have been hurt or elated by something someone said, can you share it with them, instead of fearing that you will be giving them power over you? In fact, the exact opposite is the case. The more you allow yourself to be vulnerable, the more power you are taking away from others and vesting it within yourself. For only the truly strong can afford to be vulnerable. Only the truly strong will bare their feelings without worrying if someone is going to take advantage of them.

Living vulnerably would mean crying when in grief instead of keeping a stiff upper lip. It means asking for help instead of pretending to be self-sufficient. It means admitting your weaknesses and your mistakes and owning it all. It means being okay with being human.

We are here on Planet Earth to grow as human beings. We cannot do that without occasionally faltering, falling or failing. Recognising that, forgiving ourselves for it and recouping once again is the best way we can move on.

I honestly believe there is no bigger task just now than to practice vulnerability in thought, word and action. The sooner we allow ourselves to be seen, the sooner others will do the same. If we really want to move towards a happier, healthier and more wholesome society, let us learn to embrace ourselves, warts and all, and allow ourselves to be seen. Only then will we invite intimacy into our lives.

There can be no intimacy without vulnerability. Only when we share all of ourselves can the other trust us and open up, too. How beautiful a world we can expect it to be, when we are no longer afraid of being seen, and will joyously embark on the human adventure of loving and living.

Lesson #38

Nothing We Do Is beyond Our Forgiveness

During the 16 years of depression that preceded my spiritual awakening, I had lost total faith in myself. I had completely written myself off. And yet, I, of all people, was chosen to have a spiritual awakening. I could not believe my luck. I was filled with a deep and bottomless gratitude to God for never having given up on me, even though I had done so.

God never gives up on us. We are meant to attain enlightenment, each one of us, if not in this lifetime then in the ones that follow. We are allowed infinite chances to get things right, to move on and to try again. Therefore, let us borrow a leaf from God's book and stay staunchly on our side.

I remember that in the initial stages of my awakening, it was hard to focus consistently on the happiness of the other. Try as I would, sometimes I would give in to my anger, hurt, greed and so on. At those times, I would feel really bad and would wonder if my mantra was no longer effective. The chant that brought me back to form was "All the more reason to" . The more I lost my cool, the more reason not to do so. The more I ate the wrong food, the more reason to get my diet right. The more I woke up late, the more reason to wake up on time. It seems so simple, but we are used to resisting what is wrong instead of doing what is right. I am convinced that this has much to do with poor self-esteem. The less faith and trust we have in ourselves, the more we beat up on ourselves, and the less able we are to try again.

"All the more reason" had a salutary effect on me. Instead of beating myself up in futile resistance to all the things I was doing wrong, it helped me focus on getting them right instead. "All the more reason" helped me forgive myself and to believe in myself once more. "All the more" released the energy banked in resistance and enabled me to use it to move forward instead.

But after that magical year, when all of life appeared to open for me, I lost the ability to get into the space of focussing on the other's happiness. All my mantras lost their potency, including "All the more reason". I could never get it back again, for it requires tremendous inner strength to cut through the resistance, hopelessness and despair that assail us when we simply cannot get out of the hole of addiction, or when changing a habit seems to be impossible.

Of late, though, it seems to be resonating within me once again. I am delighted. It means that I have finally reached a state where I can forgive myself easily, and that my faith in myself has grown. And that, for me, is a huge milestone.

I am pretty sure that I am not the only one who finds it hard to forgive herself. Most of us do. It is easier for us to forgive others than it is to forgive ourselves. How much we beat ourselves up for even the slightest mishap. How difficult we find it to reconcile with our errors. Is there anything more poignant than being on bad terms with oneself? Of finding no redeeming quality within us? Of losing faith in ourselves and our capacity to survive this rollercoaster called life? Of feeling disgruntled with everything in our lives and finding no satisfaction?

That is why self-forgiveness is so vital. We cannot be divided within ourselves. For that is the road to self-sabotage, unhappiness and failure. No matter what, we need to forgive ourselves. Life on Planet Earth is excruciatingly hard. Each of us has to face tough challenges. There are times we will fail ourselves, when we will do the wrong thing. We may even do terrible things and, still, we must forgive ourselves for there is no other way to redemption.

We have all lived innumerable lifetimes, and I am pretty sure we have done unimaginably horrible things. Each of us may well have raped, murdered, robbed and destroyed. None of us is above that. Still, we were given lifetimes after lifetimes to get it right. Life will not rest until we become perfect. Life is not bothered about the number of times we get it wrong. That has already been factored in because let us never forget, we have been given freedom of will. This greatest of gifts has been given only to man on Planet Earth. This means that God is willing for us to do just about anything, and yet not lose faith in our capacity to eventually get it right. That is the level of trust God has in us. And that trust still holds good today, when mankind has collectively brought the planet so close to destruction. So, forgive yourself over and over and over again. And just get back to healing, changing and growing! If God believes in us, so, too, can we.

Lesson #39

We Live in an Ethical Universe

The Universe abides by the highest standards of ethics. Wrongdoers harm themselves more than anyone else in the long run. If only this fact was as evident to the majority as it is to the wise ones, we would have a much more harmonious and honest world.

Unfortunately, the working of the Universe is not very clear to most of us, especially when our life experience is limited. We see only the surface of things, not their depth; we see only the short-term and not the long-term, and wrongly conclude that there is neither a governing force in the Universe nor a moral law. Most of us are outraged when we daily see people get away with heinous crimes simply because they have connections or wealth. When you study the scams crafted by industrialists, or see the terrible abuse of power by politicians, it is tempting to conclude that only the crafty, the cunning and the criminal succeed while the honest human is left far behind. What is the use of being good, we ask ourselves, if goodness has no power or seeming advantage? And yet, scripture after scripture admonishes you to be honest, to have integrity, to not judge, steal, betray or be unfaithful. So, are these just moral platitudes or is there some merit in being good?

From my own observation of myself, I have noticed that the consequences to wrong-doing begin the moment we commit even the smallest misdemeanour, like eating forbidden food. Our peace of mind is immediately shaken, and we begin to feel guilty. Often, in order to feel better about ourselves, we start justifying the behaviour, but the more we do that, the thicker the veil that comes between us and our conscience. This may seem too subtle an issue to bother about, but I assure you that the higher reaches of peace and happiness can only come to those whose conscience is crystal clear. Spiritual evolution is only for the guileless and the good. This is one area where no amount of money, power or fame will help. On the contrary. Freeing yourself of the ego is the only way to attain union with God, but that calls for us to rise above our narrow and selfish desires and focus on the larger good, both in big things and small.

Furthermore, the moment we choose the wrong path, we immediately deprive ourselves of the Universe's benevolence. It is not that the Universe turns away from us. Rather, it is we who turn away from the Universe. We distance ourselves so much that we no longer have access to its power. Aspirants on the spiritual path rapidly become aware of the role of the Universe in shaping and moulding their lives and circumstances. It appears that there is a vital intelligence that actively strives to help them move to the next step, and that supports them in innumerable ways. Their lives are strewn with miracles which simply cannot be explained away as coincidences. They may experience miraculous healings. When caught in a crisis, such as being stranded alone in a deserted place in the middle of the night, help comes their way through unexpected sources. Seekers have an active sense of being looked after, and of being loved. I have a weakness for food and, one time, I was thinking longingly about Sri Krishna's melt-in-the-mouth Mysorepa, when someone knocked on my door and there stood my neighbour with a couple of delicious pieces of that delicacy! Like an indulgent parent, God loves to fulfil all our wishes provided we are karmically entitled to it. But if we freewheel away from God through choosing the wrong path, these loving services are unlikely to befall us.

Because seekers know that they are co-creators of their lives along with the Universe, they strive to live in accordance with the laws of life. They strive to do the right thing as far as they are able, make amends and seek forgiveness of themselves and the other when unable to, work on going beyond their desires, do as much good to others as they can and so on. Consequently, their lives are magical, alive with all sorts of possibilities. I am pretty sure that this may not be the case with wrongdoers. Because of their ignorance with the way life works, such people believe that they are alone in a hostile or, at best, indifferent Universe, and that all progress will depend only on their unrelenting efforts. This is what often leads them down the wrong path, for they feel that they have to prioritise their welfare since there is no one else to do it.

Moreover, such a worldview is stressful and deeply alienating, often leading to a burn-out. Seekers, on the other hand, put in unrelenting effort (as the Bhagavad Gita says, that is the only thing that is in our hands), but they do more. First, they ensure that their actions are governed by the right motivation. Then, they allow themselves to be guided by the inner voice which may speak through hunches and gut feelings. Finally, having done what they can, they surrender the outcome to God. The result is that they may get their work done much more speedily, with much less effort and with much greater success. Those who are often said to have luck on their side, usually, only have good karma.

Nor can we forget that the greatest blessings on earth – loving relationships, happiness, enjoying the little things of life – will come to us only according to the proportion of goodness within us. The wrongdoers may attract awe, and sycophants but genuine love and respect? Unlikely.

Also, of course, there is the long hand of karma which diligently records our every thought, word and action and metes out to us a fate that is exactly proportionate to our karma. We get away with nothing. Actions have consequences and suffer them we must. Recently, I met Aparna, my friend Kanta's daughter, who was distraught by *her* daughter's wayward ways. I recalled that 20 years earlier, Kanta, too, had wept bitter tears on account of the many troubles Aparna had heaped upon her.

Time and time again I have noticed that those who cheat on their spouses and eventually marry another will find themselves left high and dry at some point themselves. As the Bible said with stark simplicity: What we sow, we reap.

Why, if the law is so precise, are we in ignorance of it? Precise as it may be, its timeline is often delayed. After all, the man we have killed cannot kill us in return. The woman we have raped cannot rape us back. Not in this lifetime. But, without a doubt, they can in another. Because most of our really serious crimes take time to ripen, we do not see the connection between them and the circumstances of our lives.

Sometimes, we may pay for our wrongdoing in this lifetime itself, by undergoing a really hard old age, rife with pain and all manner of suffering. Some of us are left bankrupt in our old age, despite having amassed a considerable fortune. Could this be because we earned our money the wrong way?

In short, delayed is not denied. In one lifetime or another, we shall reap the fruits of all our karma, the good, the bad and the ugly.

So, as the wise Parsis say, think good thoughts, say good words and do good actions. And enjoy the good life.

Lesson #40

Do the Right Thing

February 12, 1996: It was one of the most fraught moments of my life. I was waiting outside the eighth-floor office of Mr Nari Hira, publisher of Magna, an organisation I had spent more than five happy years with as editor of *Society*. I was meeting Mr Hira to give him my resignation.

My heart was in my mouth. After all, I had nothing in my hand. No job offer. And worse, I was not planning to look for one. I was simply jumping off the deep end. I was done with mainstream media. I was done with the consumerist philosophy that had invaded this land a couple of years back. During those years as editor of *Society*, I was privy to the blitz of marketing and promotional activities that accompanied globalisation. Simultaneously, I woke up to the realisation that promoting a culture of more and more in a planet of finite resources was a recipe for disaster. Moreover, as one on the path, it was very clear to me that chasing materialism was not the way to happiness. And, as editor of the magazine, the conflict between the values I practised and the ones I was promoting in *Society* was suffocating me.

My publisher had given me permission to work on a magazine of my vision (that's just the kind of awesome person he is!) but the advertising team had eventually advised that we not go ahead with the project. And so, here I was, making a leap into the unknown.

That night at about 8 p.m., I told my mother that I had quit my job. My mother was aghast. She did not come from the generation that threw up their jobs. My father had loyally worked with Hindustan Aeronautics Ltd (HAL) until he had retired.

But even before I could reassure her, the phone rang and I went to answer it. Parveen Chopra was on the other side. A former deputy editor at *India Today*, Parveen had come to Mumbai from Delhi four months ago to meet people for a book he was writing about the New Age in India. Having heard that I was coming out with a magazine on spirituality, he had interviewed me. But I had not heard from him since. Now, here he was calling out of the blue. And what did he want? A Mumbai correspondent for a magazine on spirituality that he was about to begin!

I remember rushing to my mother after putting down the phone, almost hysterical with relief, to tell her that I had found a job. That night, as I lay in bed, I kept taking huge deep breaths as I thanked God fervently for having spread a safety net under my feet to arrest my jump into the unknown. That experience made me realise that if you do the right thing at the right time for the right reason, you will be looked after.

Most of us tend to forget that it is God who is really running the world. We fear that we alone determine our life. And so, we play it safe too often, suppressing our dreams so that the family bread and butter is not endangered, even if we have to suppress the pricks of our conscience. But we live in an ethical Universe and if you sincerely do what is right, you will be taken care of.

A cousin took a year off from work just to be with her younger sister who had got admission in a veterinary college in Nagpur. She ignored the naysayers who told her it was suicide to let go of a safe job. A year later and back in Mumbai, she landed an extremely prestigious and well-paying job.

I have seen this played out time and again.

At the same time, if we leave the job because we could not get along with our boss or wanted more pay, the Universe does not find itself obliged to look after you. All three components are vital. You have to do the right thing, at the right time and for the right reason. If you don't get even one of these components right, you may not get the support you are looking for. A friend of mine did a course in spirituality soon after graduating from a management school. The course had such a powerful impact on her that she threw up her nascent job and looked around for something more aligned to her values. For months she struggled without any success and, eventually, went back to a corporate job. A few years later, almost by itself, she was offered a shift from sales into HR training, which was very much more her kind of thing. So, although she may have been doing the right thing, the decision was premature and, therefore, she did not get what she was looking for immediately.

In my case, even though a spiritual awakening had put me in touch with my mission to help uplift the world, I was given to understand that I could not just throw up my present job but must, instead, go through it. Thus, four years later, when I was thoroughly satiated, the urge to leave was organic and so I was supported.

Ever since this lesson came into my life, I have striven to align myself with the Universe's time cycles. I have been in relationships that were acutely uncomfortable, but I never broke away from them. Instead, I strove to learn my lessons. The result was that at some time or the other, the relationship organically dissolved, and I was set free.

I lasted for 21 whole years in my job at *Life Positive* for the same reason. I did not want to leave for the wrong reason. When the time came for me to leave, it was a clear knowing that I must now move on and vacate the chair for someone else.

And perhaps that is why there is little regret or angst over having left a powerful, influential and soul-satisfying post.

Lesson #41

Face Life, Not Death

Of the many lessons life has taught me, perhaps this is one of the most seminal. I had always wondered about the right attitude towards life and death. When death came as it inevitably must, was one supposed to peacefully pass over, or was one obliged to fight every inch of the way? I personally had no quarrel with death. To me, life on Planet Earth was a school, and the after-life was home. So why on earth would I defer going home? I always thought it was counterproductive to fight death, because no one has ultimately beaten it, though, of course, many have earned a reprieve from it.

Moreover, I also felt I lacked the dynamism to wage a battle against death. It was hard for me to move heaven and earth to save a life, as so many others around me seemed able to do.

The answer came when my mother, at the age of 91, suffered a severe stroke that paralysed her entire right side. She could neither speak nor eat. The doctors did not hold out much hope for her and told us after a week to take her back home, and to "play *bhajans*" for her until she passed away.

My sisters and I accordingly brought her home and proceeded to wait for death to take my mother. This seemed a very passive approach and I remember feeling uncomfortable about it. Just then a psychiatrist friend of mine, Dr Dayal Mirchandani, called to ask me how she was. When I told him she was on her deathbed, he said he was coming over.

Within half an hour he was sitting beside her. After examining my mother, he told me that just because she was 91 was no reason to believe that she would not recover. He said he knew of several people who had recovered at even more advanced ages. And he gave us some invaluable tips on taking care of paralysed patients. His words simply turned around my thinking a hundred per cent.

Fighting with death may be pointless, but neither must one face death. By this I mean turning one's back to life, resigning oneself to death and simply submitting. Life is precious and, therefore, one must face life till the end. Death will come when it will; none of us has the power to stop it. But one must enhance and promote the patient's life force.

This, to me, was a huge revelation. My sister Susan and I began to approach the care-giving of our mother with a new energy. We took on the services of a physiotherapist, hired a nurse and so on. In the event, my mother lived for a good two and a half years more!

This lesson has given me a new clarity about the tremendous value of life. Life is to be cherished till the last breath. There is little point in passively giving over to death. One must strive to be alive, or keep the person one is caring for alive as long as possible.

At the same time, it was clear to me that one must not fight the inevitable. If death taps on the shoulder of the invalid, step aside and give death free passage. Unlike modern medicine, which sees death as an enemy and uses aggressive intervention to fob off death, my insight only helped me to recognise that it is life one must befriend, and not death.

Even if one chooses not to take medication in a terminal case, one can still befriend life by simply enjoying whatever time one has.

This insight enabled me to heal to some extent the passivity that always came over me when I thought of fighting death. I did not have to wage war against death. Doubtless this was admirable, but I did not have what it took. But I could take other steps. I could put my focus on what possible measures I could take for healing. I could help the patient reinforce their life force. And I could keep my gaze steadily upon life.

Lesson #42

Operate from Strength, Not Weakness

I took over as editor of *Life Positive* (*LP*) in the year 2005. I had been told that we would no longer be able to pay for contributions, since a body-mind-spirit magazine is always a challenging financial venture.

Since I had skeletal staff strength, I had to find a way to manage the situation, and I struck upon one. The *LP* army of readers and seekers were an enthusiastic lot, who were eager to share their insights and experiences on the path. Hitherto, they had expressed themselves through the *Letters* page and through a section called *Sharing*, but I decided to open up the magazine to them. However, I had no intention of diluting the quality of the contents. I worked hard in the next few months to identify readers and friends who wrote well, and churned out quite a few pieces myself. The magazine looked and read well and, in time, contributions began to pour in. Even if I was stuck for matter to put in, I rejected all substandard pieces, and slowly the magazine became a place where people vied to be published, despite getting no payment for it. I used to jokingly tell them that the *LP* currency was *punya* (blessings or merit) and not *paisa* (money). And I always used the very best articles I had in each issue, resisting the temptation to hold over some for the next issue. I was confident that if I trusted God to provide the articles, She would do so.

The experience was a vindication that no matter what the situation, one had to operate from strength and not weakness. I have had many experiences with weakness as well, during my early years as editor of *LP*. I acted out of fear of losing people and, therefore, pandered to their demands, and eventually lost my power to them. I recall once that a colleague, the only one I had then, hinted that he wanted to leave in order to join a nature magazine. I begged him not to leave, and that put me in his power. A few months later, after an altercation, I told him he was free to leave the magazine, and he left. I managed the magazine on my own for a while and, to my delight and relief, I found it could be done. It was hard, but it could be done. Having established that, I no longer allowed any colleague to gain supremacy over me. And that changed my equation with them completely.

The same situation repeated itself a few years later when my mother suffered a stroke and consequently became paralysed. Unable to lift my mother up in order to feed or change her, I was entirely dependent on *ayahs* (caregivers). Naturally, almost all of them abused the situation and exploited me. It was only when a friend lent me a hospital bed that enabled me to raise and lower her through a lever that I was able to get the situation back in hand and establish the boundaries that protected my power and self-respect.

The truth is that most people will exploit situations in which they have the upper hand. Under such situations how can we take back our power?

I think one of the most important things is to recognise that the other needs us as much as we need them. The subordinate needs the job just as much as the boss needs them. The ayahs needed the job just as much as I needed them. Writers needed to be published just as much as I needed articles to publish. Often, in our powerlessness, we tend to forget this and try and retain the relationship by placating or pandering to the other. Never ever do that!

Secondly, we need to look at what would be the worst thing that could happen and accept that. This is tough, but absolutely essential if we are to stay within our power and not depend on others. One perspective that helped me hugely is to take it one day at a time. There is enough strength given to us to face any situation for a day. And daily, we renew our pledge to strive for a day. Even the hardest situation becomes bearable if we take it one day at a time.

Thirdly, we need to use the situation as an instrument for our growth. When we do this, we will eventually become strong enough to take back our power and retain it with us.

Lesson #43

Karma and Grace Go Together

The gurus will tell you, and they are absolutely right in saying so, that all events that befall us, good or bad, are karmic because our every thought, word and deed has consequences. That raises the question, what is the role of God's grace in that case? If everything is meted to us with mathematical precision based on our karma, is there any room for divine intervention?

Someone long ago had asked me this question and I had no answer to give her. But, over time, my own karmas began to unspool and I was visited with a few fairly significant challenges. It is then that I became vividly aware of the amount of grace in which we are couched when major karmic events come our way.

The first mark of grace is the time when the karmic event arrives. I have found that these challenges came to me only when I had the strength and poise to face them. The first two years after I had decided to face my conditioning were extremely debilitating. I was in such a deep spin merely processing the damage I had done to my mind that I had barely any energy to do anything else. Those years I could feel that a scaffolding had been built around me that prevented me from encountering challenging situations or people. It took several years for the scaffolding to be fully dismantled but, around 2004, the Universe decided I was ready to face life, and sent my sister a severe illness. It lasted for several months, and she eventually had to move in with my mother and me. Visiting doctors, taking her to hospitals and taking care of her took up a considerable amount of my time. What buoyed me up, though, was the realisation that I was being given an opportunity to settle accounts with my sister, for she, too, in our younger days, had nursed me devotedly through an episode of TB.

The second mark of grace is the help that comes our way when in the midst of the crisis. If we are conscious, we will become aware of the favourable circumstances that surround us. I had a wonderful doctor friend who became my mentor and guide. He never allowed me to lose hope and kept directing me to various doctors. I was also surrounded by a phalanx of loving and devoted friends who kept my spirits up by always lending me a shoulder to weep on and a ear to vent upon, even as they showered me with loving services. I remember that during a phase when I was in the hospital with my sister, with no access to home food, a dear friend surprised me with a wonderful basket of home-made food, the taste of which I still remember.

Eventually, my mentor directed us to another hospital and it is there that my sister healed. Again, the timing was uncannily infused with grace. I had just been made editor of *Life Positive*. Leaving my sister in the care of my mother and another sister, I went to Delhi to learn the ropes of production work from my departing editor, Parveen Chopra.

On my return, my sister was completely healed. The very next day, I took over charge as the new editor. The next couple of years were hectic for me at work. I worked late and returned home after 10 p.m. My sister cooked and looked after our mother, leaving me free to focus on my work. I was in awe of the impeccable timing.

These teachings became more and more pronounced as other challenges came my way. In 2009, my mother fell ill and, eventually, suffered a stroke that resulted in paralysis.

The challenge overwhelmed me initially, but even then I became conscious of the many acts of grace that fell upon me like a warm mantle. The first was the water situation. Our building had severe water cuts. Since I lived on the top floor, I often ended up getting no water at all. I quailed at the thought of looking after an invalid under such circumstances.

Miraculously, the day I brought my mother back from the hospital, our water supply was fully restored and, thereafter, until my mother passed away two and a half years later, we had no shortage whatsoever. Another tremendous act of grace was my psychiatrist friend, Dr Dayal Mirchandani's visit. I have written about it in Chapter 41, so will not elaborate on it. Suffice it to say, my sister and I had given up on our mother but he infused us with fresh hope and transformed my approach towards life and death.

Taking care of a paralysed patient is expensive, for you need an ayah, a physiotherapist and an occasional visit by a nurse or doctor. My limited salary could not stretch to meet these contingencies. But my sisters and extended family members simply stepped in and put money into my bank without my ever asking for it, until the time that my publisher magnanimously raised my salary sufficiently to enable me to manage the outgo.

In the last few months of my mother's life, her condition took a turn for the worse, and she came down with an ailment called cellulitis. Her body would be filled with pustules which would burst and discharge pus and blood, eventually turning gangrenous. Bathing and cleansing her were extremely difficult. Aruna, the nurse who had taken care of her for the past couple of years moved in with us and looked after her meticulously. But I could not afford her services for too long, and I could not get an ayah no matter how hard I tried. Finally, on Christmas Day, I prayed for the perfect ayah for my mother and dialed an obscure agency I had never tried before. In short order, Pramila came into my life – small built, neat, orderly, competent, responsible. In short, the perfect ayah. She quickly learnt how to look after my mother from Aruna, devotedly gave her acupressure treatment and plied her with homoeopathic pills three times a day, measures we had instituted as a last bid to heal her. Till my mother's dying day, Pramila looked after her as no one before her was capable of doing.

Thus, all through the long *tapasya*, grace swaddled me and enabled me to meet the challenge successfully. And that is the purpose of grace.

Karma must come to us, because that is the only way justice can prevail. But God wants us to triumph over every challenge that karma sends our way and, thereby, grow spiritually. The role of karma is to enable us to settle our accounts. Each time we do that, we grow to the next level. It is grace's job to support us in achieving this. What more proof do we need of the loving Providence that surrounds and supports us?

The third and final way that grace acts is that a lot of our karma is transmuted without us ever knowing. I have read this in the teachings of Dada Vaswani, the late spiritual head of the Pune-based Sadhu Vasvani Mission, and I believe it. If we are in line for a major accident, it might be reduced to a fractured hand or leg. If a financial debacle is to overcome us, we might face a salary cut instead. Instead of death, we might have to contend with a severe illness. And, of course, minor events may not even show up.

So, when challenges come your way, take heart. Yes, the going may be rough, but please keep your eyes peeled for grace, or, as the proverb calls it, the silver lining on the dark cloud. It will inevitably catch your eye. Know that you already have the strength to cope with it. And know that God is rooting for you.

Lesson #44

PEOPLE ARE GOOD

My mother used to be an avid viewer of Malayali soaps, which were, if such a thing is possible, even more dreadful than those in Hindi. The daughters-in-law were more scheming and manipulative, the mothers-in-law more tyrannical and despotic, and every character, with perhaps the sole exception of the hapless hero or heroine, was depraved in some way or another.

I used to attempt to discourage her from polluting our house with such garbage, but my mother resisted it spiritedly, affirming that this was just the way people were. Mass media is a powerful influencer, but all too often, it sends us the wrong message.

In my case, it was a bestseller I read during my turbulent teenage years that caused me to question the power of goodness. It was a Sidney Sheldon book which, like most of his books, revolved around a good woman who had been abused by men, and converted into an avenging angel. My fragile hope in the goodness of humanity took a savage knock, and I remember closing the book with a sense close to despair. Could goodness really not survive in the world?

Now, you might wonder why I would place my faith in a populist writer whose purpose was to sell his books, but when you are looking to understand life, and you are the bookish kind of person I was, you look to books to teach you about life. What did I, leading a sheltered life in a tiny township in Orissa, know about life? Looking back, I am sure there are countless kids like me who get their initial cues about life from books. Ever since then, I have regretted the opportunism of populist writers who project a cynical view of life simply to sell books.

My faith in goodness took a further beating when I was about 27 or so, and living with my sister in a Mumbai co-operative housing society. One of its members, let us call him A, used to advertise his flat in the rentals section of the papers and take an initial deposit from interested parties. When the day came for them to move in, his wife would open the door, tell them that it was she who owned the flat and not A, and refuse to allow them to enter. The man himself would be nowhere to be seen.

Inevitably, the enraged renters would create row upon row, with very little effect on A. Eventually, fed up of the situation, some of the building boys dragged A down to the ground floor where the rest of the residents decided to confront him. To my chagrin, A's blazing insolence overrode all the objections raised by the residents until everyone fell silent. It was left to another man, rumoured to be a smuggler, to sternly put the offender in his place and forbid him from becoming a nuisance to the society. I could not help wonder at the impotence of the supposedly 'good' people!

Fortunately, a spiritual awakening gave me a fresh understanding of what goodness actually was. Goodness was the capacity to prioritise the welfare of the other. It was the capacity to rise above one's ego consistently. It was simultaneously a refusal to allow wrongdoing to carry the day, for wrongdoing was not in the best interests of anyone. I learnt to lovingly refuse to allow the bully or the manipulator to use me, not for my sake, but for their own. My commitment to their welfare compelled me to ensure that they behaved as well as they could, for nothing else was in their welfare. This continued until the effect of the transformation left me and I was back to being my hyper-reactive self.

But the insights I had gleaned remained and gave me a profound understanding of life.

Through my own exploration into the nature of the Self, I also discovered that each of us were innately whole and perfect, the epitome of goodness. It was our conditioning – all the wounds and viewpoints about ourselves, others and life, that accounted for our less-than-perfect behaviours. But all we had to do was to free ourselves of our conditioning, and our perfect self would be revealed.

This redoubled my faith in humanity and I became convinced that people were innately good. Which, of course, was diametrically opposite to the message mass media was broadcasting, thanks to their credo: Bad News Sells.

Thus, day after day, we are exposed to nothing less than a Rogue's Gallery of murderers, terrorists, rapists, thieves, scamsters and so on. Years of being exposed to this inevitably cause us to nurse the same suspicion I did as a teenager – that goodness does not have a chance to survive against the chicanery of humanity! That in the battle between good and bad, it is bad that carries the day.

Unfortunately, we then begin to operate from that thought, and view our fellow human beings with suspicion and fear. Because we create our reality through our feelings and thoughts, we will indeed attract the very behaviours we are resisting. Most of the people we meet will betray our trust, thereby convincing us of the truth of our convictions. Who loses if I go around thinking that the world is full of vile abusers and manipulators? Surely, myself? The other goes his merry way, but not only am I meeting villain after villain but am getting trapped in a worldview that will torpedo my happiness and my own goodness. My journalist colleagues have little idea of how seminally they are, in fact, changing the world for the worse because of the belief that bad news sells.

However, even if we are busily creating the illusory world the mass media sells us, we still have not gone so down the road that we inhabit that world in our everyday lives. In other words, every second person we meet is, thankfully, still not a murderer, rapist or terrorist. In fact, a trip I made to Chokhi Dhani (a fair consisting of a reconstructed Rajasthani village) in Jaipur gave me a good yardstick to gauge humanity by. One of the stalls in that village held an attractive collection of trinkets and baubles. I asked the owner how many people stole from his shop. He told me 80 per cent were honest, and 20 were not. To me, this is a measure of humanity itself. 80 per cent, or perhaps even more, are honest. 20 may not be. I can live with these odds. The world is safe with 80 per cent being on the side of goodness. And, after all, it could not be otherwise. It is only because the vast majority is decent, honest, interested only in earning a living, taking care of their family and being happy, that the world still exists. If the majority were evil, the world would have surely collapsed.

So, be of stout heart and venture into the world confidently. The world is safe. People are innately good. In the battle against good and bad, goodness wins, because that is who we are. And when you factor in karma and recognise that we get our just deserts sooner or later, we can indeed be sure that virtue rules!

Lesson #45

The Body Heals Itself

As one who has contended with many ailments, while still operating from the premise that I am innately whole and perfect, it was an article of faith with me that health was who I truly was, and all the many ailments that embroiled me in discomfort and dis-ease were merely imposters who would take themselves off the moment this insight became a felt reality.

Having subjected my mind and my body to a close study during all my various malaises, I have discovered that resistance to them is an ongoing experience. I may not even be particularly conscious of it, but underlying all that I am thinking or doing is a low-grade negativity consisting of the discomfort the ailment brings in its wake, my fear and anxiety about its impact on my body and life, my angst lest I not heal and a lurking dread that I might die. This negativity tightens all the cells in my body. As Anju Venkat of The Health Awareness Centre (THAC), a revolutionary healing organisation founded by the legendary Vijaya Venkat, explained to me, in the face of fear, anxiety or any negative emotions, the cell walls in the body shut down, and all interaction and cooperation among each other ceases. How truly disastrous.

I have also noticed that when I am anxious, my breathing is shallow because my diaphragm tightens, and all prana to the bottom half of my body, especially to my all-important abdomen, ceases to flow. Therefore, the more relaxed and joyous I am, the more naturally I will regain my health.

At various times and in various ways, this realisation has proved itself through many spontaneous healings.

In 2008, I began to run a fever that lasted five days without let up. Far from being perturbed, I welcomed it, for my Ayurvedic doctor had told me that my immunity was so low that my body was not capable of even getting a fever. I interpreted my fever to mean that my immunity had hiked up. But after the 5th day, I decided to consult my family doctor. He immediately pressed the alarm button, insisted that I test for a number of ailments and I was diagnosed with typhoid. I called up a couple of evolved friends, asked them to send me healing and then took to my bed with a rare composure. It was a mild attack, for my appetite was unimpaired and I experienced no discomfort whatsoever. In time, not only did I heal but the illness seemed to have got rid of a great deal of toxins because my hair looked glossy, my complexion improved, I began to sleep better and, best of all, the arthritic pain in my knees totally disappeared. The fever, perhaps, had really spring-cleaned my system, assisted by my own relative peace of mind.

In 2009, my mother had fallen very badly ill with cerebral malaria and was hospitalised. At that point, I had been contending with a newly discovered allergy for wheat and dairy, which were the main cause of an asthmatic condition. Deeply concerned that my food addiction was endangering me, I was in an endemic state of fear. However, my mother's grave condition forced me to focus on her. I remember telling my body each time some tendril of worry or anxiety pushed its way in, "Body, I cannot worry about you just now. You will just have to cope with the situation on your own."

Naturally, this was just what the body was waiting to hear because, in a week or so, I began to experience perfect wellness. Although I was sleeping very little and spending most of my time with my mother in the hospital, I found that I could eat all sorts of things I could earlier not, including biscuits, fried items and fermented food, without breaking into a cold or congestion. My challenged digestive system began to rectify itself and I was able to eat anything and everything. The *uttapams* I ordered from a nearby hotel and delightedly consumed were countless! Having lost a great deal of weight earlier, to my joy I found that I was putting it back on again.

Of course, the moment my mother came home again and life became more routine, I had more time to worry and my illnesses came home to roost!

In 2014, I went on a holiday to South Africa along with my sister Leela, to spend some time with her daughter, Deepa. I was full of anxiety on account of my health because I had recently contracted Irritable Bowel Syndrome (IBS) and I was unsure how I would manage the ailment when I would not be able to control the food I ate. Moreover, I was suffering from extremely bad sinus which was making me feel giddy and nauseous. And, finally, my sciatica (a pain that radiates from one's bottom all the way to the ankles) was acting up.

The holiday was a hectic one. We were on the move virtually every day, for my niece and her husband were determined to show us as much of their beautiful country as they possibly could. Piled up in their car, my sister and I would laugh and joke with my niece's adorable two daughters. Moreover, we would drive for exceedingly long hours in the interest of reaching our destination on time, without taking a break. After an early breakfast, lunch would usually be partaken at 3 p.m. or 4 p.m. The long break gave my stomach the chance to repair itself, and the genial company enabled me to forget my ailments. Suffice it to say that at the end of the holiday, my stomach was much better, I had gained a couple of much-needed kgs of weight, my sinus had disappeared and, as for my sciatica, I seemed to have left it permanently behind in South Africa!

Sometime in 2018, it became more and more clear to me that I was Spirit and not matter. As Spirit, I was the likeness of God and, therefore, absolute health, among a whole lot of other absolute attributes. The more I began to affirm this, the healthier I got and, once again, my illnesses began to recede. Unfortunately, I would always overdo my indulgence in forbidden food, relapse into guilt and fear and the illnesses would creep back once again.

All this has led me to the firm conviction that the body has the innate capacity to heal itself, if only I can cultivate the discipline of not thinking about my ailments.

As a matter of fact, I have been nursing a cold that became a chest congestion while writing this piece. Reminding myself of the truth of this insight, that I was health and not illness and that the fears and worries that were slowly crippling me since this morning were illusory, slowly healed me. I have thrown up some phlegm, my chest feels better and any anxiety about being up for a long-drawn illness is dissipating!

Indeed the body can heal itself. Just step out of the way!

Lesson #46

Focus on What Works

My publisher, Mr Nari Hira, in the Magna group where I worked as editor of *Society* magazine, was a remarkable man, who I have the highest respect for. One of his many wonderful attributes was his capacity to simply step out of the way of his editors and allow them to run the magazine as they thought fit. I can hardly recall even one instance of Mr Hira interfering in the editorial content or, indeed, in anything else either.

But what I cherished most about Mr Hira was the remarkable wisdom with which he managed me. Each time I came out with a good issue, he would praise it lavishly. If the issue was not as good as it could be, he simply said nothing.

What did this policy do for me? It built up my confidence. It made me feel appreciated. It inspired me to do better.

Most of us do the exact opposite. When our underlings, domestic staff, family members or even the world at large perform laudably, we fail to reach out and tell them so, convincing ourselves that too much praise will go to their heads. On the other hand, if the wife were to forget to put sugar in the coffee, or the children were to raise mayhem while your boss was on the line or the maid was to take leave without giving notice, you would definitely rave and rant without a second thought.

Well, you can't help it. It is human nature to take the positive for granted and resist the negative. We take the perfect working of the human body for granted but should something go wrong, even if it is a tiny cut on the finger, we can't seem to stop thinking about it.

However, psychologists say that if you want people to change, appreciate them fulsomely when they do the right thing; something that Mr Hira did. When they relapse into the behaviour you are trying to correct, you should cultivate the self-control to say nothing.

It is very hard. When things go wrong, it is only human to holler. But it is counterproductive. As they say in spiritual circles, energy flows where attention goes. The more you focus on what does not work, the more you reinforce it. You need to direct your attention to what works because only that will reinforce the behaviour. Doing this consistently can bring many breakthroughs for you and for those around you.

You could even consider adopting this practice with your own self. For we are even more intolerant of our own goof-ups. Next time you want to change a habit or entrenched behaviour pattern, appreciate yourself generously each time you remember to do the right thing. You need to reinforce that within yourself. When you repeat the unwanted behaviour, forgive yourself and recommit to changing yourself.

I have been a food addict for several years now, and it has been a really long and difficult journey because of my wheat and milk allergy. Sometimes, it gets too tempting to break the rules, especially when it comes to sweets and biscuits. But, over the years, my capacity to endorse the times when I abide by the rules and to ignore the times that I don't, is healing my addiction from inside out. Yes, I still have a way to go but I am far better than I used to be. I am learning to prioritise health and fitness over taste and I am confident that, in time, food will have no power over me.

This principle applies to the larger world as well. Most of us cannot resist criticising and carping about all the things going wrong in the world. Social media is a particularly fraught avenue for venting, where trolling and vicious personal attacks are exchanged on the basis of one's political affiliation or the religion one subscribes to. The newspapers, too, consistently write about all that is going wrong in the world while never appearing to notice the many things quietly going right. We, at *Life Positive*, consistently practised focussing on what worked, and refused to write about the many scandals some gurus found themselves embroiled in. When it came to book reviews, we simply did not write about the books we could not endorse. What was the point of directing publicity at something that did not deserve it? Criticising something is the best way of drawing people's attention to something.

Focussing on what works and not on what does not work is a powerful spiritual principle that is difficult to practice only because it goes against the human tendency to protest loudly against what does not work. It, therefore, requires a lot of inner work to get to a stage where one can mute one's protests and turn one's attention consistently on what you want to bring about in your life or in the lives of others.

The Buddha was able to transform Angulimala simply because of his focus on who Angulimala really was, as opposed to the person he appeared to be.

Jesus Christ transformed Mary Magdalene on the same grounds. The great gurus know that we are souls and not the faulty minds and bodies we think we are. Therefore, their focus is always on the limitless potential within, not on what our behaviour labels us to be.

True compassion, both towards oneself and others, is about appreciating when they do the right thing and being forbearing when they do not.

Lesson #47

Say Yes to Every Opportunity

I have been practising the principle of saying yes to every opportunity that came my way over the last decade, and although nothing spectacular has shown up – like being invited to tea at the Rashtrapati Bhavan or receiving the Nobel Peace Prize – my life has been greatly enriched by this practice.

I have just returned from a lovely long trip to Tamil Nadu because I said yes to giving a talk to a ladies' organisation in Trichy, and to holding a writer's workshop for some teachers and students in Madurai. On my own, I would never have gone to these places in all likelihood, but the word 'yes' got me there.

In the course of running my workshops, I have said yes to almost every opportunity that came my way, which has included training a corporate honcho, teaching some government servants, giving talks to women and training students and teachers. Each time these opportunities came my way, my heart has fluttered and I have experienced the scary feeling of having to go beyond my comfort zone. But that is exactly what makes it so exciting. Saying yes consistently takes us into the uncharted zone of the unknown and helps us coast along the path of evolution and growth.

I am firmly of the conviction that all the opportunities strewn along our path come from the Universe and, therefore, we had better not say no to them, for who knows what mysterious or mighty doors will open with the word 'yes'?

A friend of mine called me out of the blue, and told me she wanted me to adopt a kitten she had been fostering. Her words seemed like the voice of God to me, so I said yes, although I had no previous experience of looking after a cat, nor did I like them very much. What a life-changing experience it turned out to be, for not only was it my first experience at caregiving, but it also opened me up to the whole animal world which I had not really been attuned to. After opening the doors of my house and heart to my pet, Kutta, I could no longer look away indifferently any time I saw an animal in distress. I became an abiding cat lover and, although Kutta exited from this world a few years back at the grand age of 15 and a half, every cat I ever see has my allegiance.

When my former *Life Positive* publisher gave me the munificent gift of a return ticket to Canada and the US with a stopover in London, I was overwhelmed with gratitude, but also acutely uncomfortable. I had travelled very little, and here I was expected to travel on my own halfway around the world at the age of 60! It was a scary prospect, especially as my health began to act up at the time, but I courageously said yes and opened the doors to a most wonderful and exciting holiday, which also helped me slay many fears.

It is only by saying yes to the opportunities given to us, and doing our very best with them, that we pave the way to our own success and destiny. For life happens one step at a time and when we sincerely do our best at each step, that itself will create the next step.

Those of us who are too fearful to say yes, may miss the boat quite a few times. But never fear. The doors are never closed to us. The Universe will never give up on us. So don't let the earlier nays stop you from say aye this time if you feel ready to.

It is, at the same time, equally true that opportunities will begin to falter and drop if we keep closing our minds to them and shaking our heads each time they dangle invitingly before us. My sister was at the bank when a young woman approached her and told her that she looked like an elegant older woman and that she would like to cast her in a TV serial. My sister, unfortunately, said no and thereby closed the door to goodness knows what exciting possibilities, especially as she had been a gifted actor in her school and college days.

Of course, we should say yes only if we feel internally ready. If we do not, the event may end in a disaster and discourage us from taking further risks. Starting my little entrepreneurial venture of holding writing workshops, or even leaving *Life Positive*, both involved risks, but my inner voice said I was ready and, so, I took the plunge.

I need hardly say that one should say yes only to ethical and legal opportunities. Please do not say yes to anyone writing in from Nigeria offering you a million dollars if you would only give them your bank details!

The more we learn to say yes, the more comfortable we become with the unknown, and the bolder and more confident we become in courting it. Eventually, we will also learn to say yes to the challenges life throws at us and, in time, begin to unconditionally embrace the adventure of living. We can, for instance, learn to say yes to failure, to a health scare or a divorce. Yes, they are not pleasant, but they are there, and our not accepting it can only make our lives more difficult. Saying yes to problems will give us the strength to focus on what we can do about the situation, and to look for the opportunities it contains. Above all, it will give us the tranquillity and inner invincibility to take the situation in our stride and not be diminished as human beings. And that, after all, is the point of living.

Lesson #48

Keep No Secrets

Blessed is the one whose life is an open book. He or she has nothing to fear from anyone at all. The reverse is also true. If he or she fears not public sanction, they are free to lead their life as an open book.

No matter where it begins, it is a wonderful idea to lead a life with no skeletons in the cupboard. No matter what you have done, or has been done to you, can you face it, heal from it and have the capacity to share it with others so that it has no power over you?

For most of us, the idea is horrifying, even when we have, generally, been on the right side of the law. Our faults and fallacies won't land us in jail, though they may cost us our good image in the eyes of others. But one thing is for sure. The more we hide these issues, perhaps a drinking problem, an eating disorder, dyslexia or cancer, the more power they have over us. The more we fear being exposed, the bigger the problem gets in our own eyes. Furthermore, because we tend to not share it with others, we deny ourselves the help we may get from other sources to finally heal from the issue.

Soon, these secrets may become so inflated that they start to affect us severely. We might withdraw from people in order to cover up this part of our life; maybe we begin to limit our confidences even with the people we love the most or maybe we resort to lies. No matter which of these choices we make, the result is unhealthy, pushing us further into the power of this guilty secret.

There are some who keep secrets because it makes them feel important. It makes them happy to deny others access to that knowledge because, in their eyes, knowledge is power. Hence, they, too, may choose to lie instead of speaking the truth and, thereby, not only invite complications into their lives but cause them to live on bad terms with their conscience. Not only that, there are so many other consequences to keeping secrets. Keeping bad faith with others will cost you their trust, and also intimacy in the relationship. It will add baggage to your life that you simply do not need.

Learning to speak the truth and freeing yourself of the toxic impact of rancid secrets is a bit of a process. You need to cultivate the courage to bare yourself.

A friend of mine who was part of a group of six people, once shared with us that her marriage was a sham and that her husband was having an extra-marital affair with his colleague. It took us all time to digest this for we had always thought that the marriage was an exceptionally healthy one. But once the truth was out, my friend found our group the one place where she could be herself, talk about the pain she was enduring and weep unabashedly. Eventually, this gave her the courage to confront her husband and force him to choose between her or his colleague. The husband chose her, but my friend insisted that they would have to go to a marriage counsellor and heal their marriage before she was willing to commit herself. He happily agreed, and now finally the stars are back in my friend's eyes and her husband, too, is finding her company more and more restful and joyous. Her confrontation brought their relationship to the conscious level and enabled them to work on it.

So, lose no time in sharing with those you need to, so that you can free yourself. You don't have to share it with the world. Just with those who need to know. I agree it is tough, and you should do it only when you feel ready to do so.

At the same time, there are certain issues that need to be handled with great delicacy and even discretion. Telling your spouse that you have had an extra-marital relationship may have radical consequences. Are you willing to accept them? How can you ensure that the revelation will not explode your marriage? If the affair is over and done with and you are back with your spouse, should you even share it? Consider before talking about it.

If you have adopted a child, it is a very tricky question whether you should tell the child or not. Either way, there could be negative consequences, so tread carefully.

Use your wisdom to help you chart out your course towards reducing the number of secrets you are hoarding. Often, your confidences may not come as a surprise to your listener. We give away much more than we can imagine through our expressions, body language and state of being. So, why not let it out?

Personally, I would rather share everything about my life than keep things stuffed inside of myself and worry about other people getting to know about it. I consciously work on being open and transparent in all areas of my life. I openly share my weaknesses, failures or the events that show me in a poor light. I am okay to take the shroud off my dark side, for I know that only then will I be truly seen and even loved.

I like to think that my friendships gain from this transparency and that my friends trust me because they know that I am no sham.

I hope we are all aware that this point only works with our own secrets and not with the secrets of others. I like to lead my life as an open book, but that does not mean I will share others' secrets with the world. Those secrets do not belong to me, and breaking a confidence is to break trust.

Finally, what if you have done something seriously wrong, such as rape or theft? My advice would be to own it up. Go to the police and confess, and accept the consequences. Use the situation to learn your lessons. Burying the truth in your mind has serious karmic consequences, if not in this lifetime, then in another. Never ever believe that you get away with anything. Sooner or later, karma will surely hunt you out. It may be in another lifetime, but it will still be you paying the price.

Remember that we live in an ethical Universe. So, align yourself with it and own up. Life and God will forgive you, though it will not spare you the karmic consequences of the action. Learn to forgive yourself, too, and become a better human being.

Lesson #49

Get Inspired

I have been listening to the lovely classic song, "*Insaf ki dagar pe, bachon dikhao chal ke*," which exhorts children to walk the path of justice, to bear the hardships of life without uttering a whimper, strengthened only by Truth and to never falter, no matter how harrowing the path, because they will eventually change the world.

The more I listen to it, the more these fervent words move me, and I wonder why education could not be more focused on drawing the best out of the child, by believing in him or her and inspiring them by filling them with the highest ideals.

Is there anything more powerful than inspiration to motivate us? To direct children towards prosaic goals such as money or power is doing them a great injustice. The human soul vibrates at a much higher pitch, and songs such as these give meaning and purpose to life while pointing us to a much loftier destiny than we would get by merely cavorting in the funfair of materialism.

Personally, I am convinced that inspiration can unlock our highest potential and drive us to superhuman achievements. All the great souls have been inspired by some ideal or cause that enables them to sacrifice all that the common man holds dear such as comfort, leisure, family and, very often, life itself. Nelson Mandela, Martin Luther King, Abraham Lincoln, Mother Teresa, Ramakrishna

Paramahansa, Ramana Maharishi, were all inspired by great ideals and, in turn, have been great inspirations to the world.

We only have to think of Mahatma Gandhi to recognise what a powerful quality inspiration can be. By virtue of his own courage of conviction, his transparent sincerity, the rightness of his principles and his unflinching adherence to them, he galvanised a whole country consisting of ordinary farmers, traders, housewives, factory workers, weavers and clerks to steadfastly abide by the principles of non-violent resistance despite being assailed by the bullets and batons of the British. The capacity to withstand violence without responding with violence calls for tremendous self-control and forbearance. How did our *aam aadmi* (common man) rise to such levels? Because Gandhiji believed it was possible for them to do so, and he modelled that possibility for them.

All of us, in our heart of hearts, hunger for significance, to touch some part of greatness within ourselves, to strive for a cause greater than us. When we meet someone capable of igniting this within us, we awaken the best in us. Who would imagine that Vinobha Bhave, the great follower of Mahatma Gandhi, could actually inspire people to give up massive tracts of land in order to benefit those who had none? Vinobha Bhave's Bhoodan Movement, whose practitioners went around the country exhorting landowners to give some part of the land to the dispossessed, remains another testimony to the greatness that lies in the depths of each human being, and which can come to life under the influence of inspiration.

How does inspiration work its magic? It does it by broadcasting insights that we already dimly know to be the truth. It also appeals to the best in all of us, the soul that lurks inside us, silent and still, but which is powerfully affected by great thoughts, words and actions. Meeting people who model the values or mission that they seek to kindle within us is also a surefire way of spreading the flame.

Inspiring leaders have a powerful mission and vision that they are possessed by. They are coherent in their value system. They strive to eliminate anything that is not aligned with their values or to the destination that they are wedded to. Their presence is potent with character, integrity and authenticity. No one can fake inspiration. There are charismatic leaders who can use the power of their personality to hypnotise and entice, but sooner or later the scales will fall from the eyes of the disciples. But the inspiring leader is not after power or fame. She does not seek the adulation of her disciples. She is far above using the cult of personality. Her power derives from nothing but naked adherence to the principles and values she believes in. She can be banked upon.

As one who has travelled and stayed in many ashrams, I have seen the power of inspiration in practice. I still recall going to the Brahma Kumari Headquarters in Mount Abu and interviewing some of the volunteers and workers there. I met a young accountant, whose eyes glowed when he talked about the joy he got in serving the Sisters (the organization is led by women leaders) who looked after him with so much love. His average working day stretched to more than 11 to 12 hours, but he claimed that he never felt tired. I also met some women rolling rotis to serve the youth delegation that had descended upon the ashram in large numbers. The man in charge of them turned up around lunchtime and asked them if they would rather have lunch or continue to do *seva* (service). In one voice, the women opted for seva.

In ashram after ashram, I have seen this dogged devotion to duty, where without heed to time or effort, disciples pour their energy into the task of the moment. Around the time of Sri Sri Ravi Shankar's 50th birthday celebration, I had gone to their Bangalore ashram to profile the guru. The devotees were mostly young people or the well-heeled. Even here, enthusiasm and love for the guru charged them with a tremendous purpose. I found many of them involving themselves in village uplift, organic farming, building toilets for rural households and holding reconciliation talks between warring factions.

I often wondered if some of the people I met at ashrams who sparkled so with dynamism and intention were the same who warmed the seats of government offices, waiting only for retirement and the pension!

I would not be surprised if they were, and to that I can only say one thing. Maybe government organisations ought to spend some time inspiring their employees to serve their fellow countrymen. After all, they have no other motivation than seva, for their jobs are pretty much secure and what could be a higher purpose than to look after all the millions who so sorely need their help?

The corporate world has been quick to grasp the power of inspiration, and most organisations have a mission and vision statement drawn up. Unfortunately, somewhere down the line, they fail the coherence test, for their profit motive eventually causes them to part company with the lofty values they are supposed to adhere to.

My faith in the power of inspiration is drawn from my own experience. Despite being deeply idealistic, nothing moved me because I could not find a cause I could identify with. It was the awakening that galvanised me into life. Life became full of meaning and purpose, and the idea of supporting people into leading holistic lives which would eventually pave the path for the Spiritual Age became a mission that has, since, never stopped inspiring me. Thinking of it is enough to bring tears into my eyes. Whatever I have done since my awakening in 1991 has always been with this purpose in mind.

Money, fame or power, have never had the power to drive me. Inspiration and only inspiration is capable of doing that. This must be true of the vast majority of people who today languish hopelessly, unable to find the trigger that can move their souls. As many thinkers have pointed out, we are facing a crisis of meaning in our lives. In the wasteland of materialism in which we are all steeped in presently, it is hard to find a cause that can make us come alive.

Ultimately, we need to seek no further than our own selves for an abiding source of inspiration. When we can withdraw our senses from the lure of the material world and tune within, we will find all the truths of life there. We will find God, ourselves and the other. And that is enough to keep us inspired lifelong.

Lesson #50

Serve Life

Once in a while, a nugget of insight surfaces that acts like a touchstone to measure everything by. This happened to me while writing the piece about women in this book (Chapter 31). I rhetorically asked the question what woman's work consisted of and concluded that it was about giving and sustaining life. In a flash, it occurred to me that nothing could be more important than life.

It is odd how easy it is to lose sight of the truly important. The ego does a good job of it. And, therefore, we tend to believe that going to the office to sell a million tubes of toothpaste, or working in a lab to discover the secrets of science, or building mammoth skyscrapers, are far more important than bringing up children, keeping the peace between feuding siblings or growing plants. These don't need a special education for one thing, and even illiterate peasants can do it, so obviously they can't amount to much is the conclusion the ego comes to.

It is not that the former tasks are not important. It is just that they cannot be the highest priority. The highest priority has to be the caretakership of life in as many ways as we possibly can because that is what Planet Earth consists of – life.

Anything we do that endangers life in any way gives us the signal that we are acting wrongly. It is breathtakingly frightening to assess our present system by these parameters because almost everything we do is anti-life. Modern medicine and modern farming are both anti-life, for their approach is to kill and destroy.

To give another example of an anti-life approach, we need not look further than science. Scientists keep arriving at conclusions which they have to revise five years down the line, and inventing products that inevitably have side-effects on some part of the Universe.

Our consumerist lifestyle is the biggest example of a system which is anti-life, for the unbridled production, consumption and discarding of countless goods and products is destroying Planet Earth, polluting the air, water and soil, killing thousands of species, despoiling the resources of Mother Earth and provoking climate change and water crisis.

Even so, for the last several decades, politicians and economists have only focused on the economy as the single most important component of their manifesto. To keep the economy flourishing and to continuously amp up the level of growth year after year appear to be the Holy Grail of all politicians anywhere. Is this even possible? Nothing in nature grows continuously. Every rise has a proportionate fall. Before economists began to tinker with the economy, people were still buying and selling goods, though in a much more moderate manner, and there was no recession either. It is only after the economy became a science that recession became a phenomenon.

Today, most governments focus primarily on sustaining the economy. When the Corona Virus descended upon us, many governments prioritised the economy over human lives, by continuing business as usual. So, why is the economy considered so important? Because all of us have become accustomed to our lives of plenty, and the idea that anything can topple the dream of more and more is so frightening that politicians would rather face anything than the wrath of the people. Besides, the collapse of the economy will mean crippling job losses and a descent into a vicious cycle that will spiral down to a depression. A scary prospect, doubtless, but surely less grave than the loss of species, calamitous climate change and the collapse of Planet Earth? What would you rather have – collapse of the economy or that of Planet Earth? What are you more likely to survive? Right now, with the onset of the Corona Virus, the choice has been taken out of our hands as economies everywhere tank, and millions of businesses worldwide have closed down.

System after system, whether we are talking about architecture, education or nutrition, are all anti-life. Why so? The answer is simple. Modern civilisation is based on a separatist, fragmentary understanding of life, whereas we live in an interconnected world. Everything we think, speak and do has an impact on the larger whole. Oneness is the truth of our existence and, therefore, when we destroy one part of Creation, it has its impact on all parts of Creation. Unless we understand this truth and abide by its law, we will continue to wreak havoc with our every system and invention, while ironically referring to the mayhem we leave behind as progress.

I am convinced that if our focus was on the larger good rather than the profit motive, we will find it easier to arrive at solutions that work for everyone and everything. No longer will we have to cringe about our shampoos and soaps destroying forests in order to grow oil palm trees. No longer will we have to think about our carbon footprint each time we take a plane or drive our private cars. No longer will we have to worry about what eating a carrot or an apple will do to our insides. No longer will we have to worry about plastics destroying the planet.

In today's times, none of us can be truly happy because everything is conflicting with everything else. How can we be happy knowing everything we do is destroying some aspect or other of our priceless planet? This way of life is not sustainable, my dear friends. We need to wake up from the drug of desire that is killing us softly.

What if we were to prioritise life and let the economy go hang? Most of us will suffer, perhaps for a long time but, in the long run, maybe we will be able to recalibrate our lives on a more holistic foundation, learn to live without, and use our energies in creative tasks and community building when not looking after life. Maybe in time, our water, air and soil will revive and, with it, the return of the species. Anything that challenges the longevity of our planet or the lives of our mineral, plant or animal brothers and sisters, cannot be good for us in the long run. The Corona Virus, I believe, is doing just that. None of us know what kind of a world is going to be left behind after the Corona is done with it. But in all probability, the Economy will be in a shambles.

Similarly, if we were to relook at all our systems through the lens of Oneness, we will finally find the happiness and harmony that we long for. Not just us, but everything on Planet Earth, too. For one thing, scientists must all become sages first, and only then arrive at any conclusions about earth and life. Economists need to take their mind off the profit motive and seek to serve all of life. Farmers need to grow food that is wholesome and healthy, as they once did. All of us should consider ourselves at the service of life, if we want our own lives to flourish.

Supporting and sustaining life begins with ourselves. We are obliged to do all that it takes to burnish our own lives. This would mean healing from old wounds, releasing ourselves from our limitations, expanding and realising our potential, maintaining our boundaries with others, ensuring that we are treated right, and becoming the magnificent beings we are meant to be.

It also means supporting others to do the same. Let us tell each other our stories, appreciate each other, celebrate each other, help one another and love one another. Through the perspective of Oneness, we can finally arrive at heaven on earth.

Epilogue

This book has been born of my firm conviction that life really begins to yield its richest rewards as we grow older. In my own case, it has been absolutely true that life grew in achievements, wisdom, character and understanding as I grew older. Having crossed the threshold of 60 in June 2017, I find myself infinitely more peaceful, happy and successful. Life seems to be getting sweeter by the moment. Yes, problems crop up. Things do not always go my way. Bitter disappointments occasionally shatter me. No matter what, I find myself eventually swinging back to the mean, with perhaps a few lessons learnt or some adjustments made. I have the sense that I am growing ongoingly, and that I am becoming a stronger, more accepting and less resisting person in every way. The Suma who wakes up in the morning is a shade better than the Suma who went to bed last night.

This vision of life as an expansive unfoldment is not how most of us perceive ourselves or old age. We believe that life is most glorious in our youth – that golden period between 16 and 32, and then it steadfastly declines, until it peters out into a gloomy and decrepit old age. I, of course, cannot speak for what lies on the other side of 60. Certainly, I am keenly aware of the deprivations and difficulties that confront many in their old age, as their senses begin to close down, they cease to have control over their bodies and sicknesses mount. At the same time, I personally know hundreds of vigorous, healthy and contributing individuals who emanate unbroken energy and drive. These people are often still healthy, still working, still driving, still cooking, still travelling, still relating, still fully paid up human beings, and I take heart from them.

Even better, and perhaps this is where old age uniquely scores, is that they seem to have got their act together. They seem to know who they are, what they are moving towards and what truly matters. Their movements are no longer hurried, but purposeful. They are more spacious in themselves and are, therefore, able to give themselves and those around them more leeway. Their very energy draws people to them, who draw a bit of the elders' lived wisdom to fuel their own life journey.

The old age we reap is the sum total of the life we have led so far. If we lead balanced lives, look after our bodies, engage in meaningful work, work relentlessly on becoming a better version of ourselves every day, do as much good as we possibly can and expiate our karmas, we may reliably expect to have a happy old age. It may have its share of bodily discomforts but will in no way stop us from leading a happy, healthy, active and even creatively charged life.

So, while I cannot speak for life beyond 60, I can confidently speak for life up to 60. It's been great. And I both hope and intend that it should get even greater. Why my life seems to have opened up in breadth and depth as the years went by, I believe, is because somewhere along the way, I learnt the secrets of leading a successful life. I must clarify that, in my book, a successful life is not a life studded with star-spangled achievements, but a life that has been lived in scrupulous adherence to the laws of life. A life in which one walks hand in hand with the Creator, co-creating a beautiful tapestry in which everything is woven with balance and proportion, relationships, work, health, self-work, creativity and contribution to society.

This book encapsulates some of the life lessons that have enabled me to lead my life this far. They have enabled me to overcome the difficulties that life threw at me successfully, they have helped me to heal relationships and to grow out of them, they have helped me to transition towards work that is both meaningful and creatively rewarding and they have helped me to retain my innocence, faith, love and trust in God, man and myself.

My intention for the book is that you should be able to implement these lessons in your own life and to also feel within yourself the possibility of a life that expands ongoingly with age and not contracts. I hope and pray that your life unfurls with every day.

Corona Lessons

My book was written before the Novel Coronavirus made its spectacular appearance in November 2019. By the end of March 2020, India, and much of the world, was under lockdown, and the world had changed in the most surreal and unimaginable way. It is almost as if the Universe had pulled the plug off normal existence and, presto, life mutated in every possible way.

The virus has chased most humans across the world indoor. Work-from-home has become the norm for those who can do it. Many others have been simply forced to stop working. These include much of unorganised labour as well as domestic staff. For the first time ever, most of middle-class India is forced to clean up its own mess in the absence of domestic help. In another first, men are chipping in with sweeping and swabbing, dishwashing and some cooking, as well. Even children, driven home like everyone else, have been helping out with home chores. Eating out has stopped. Healthy home-cooked food has become the only option. Families are bonding over board games, sing-song sessions and storytelling.

With time, the lockdown has had a punishing effect on the economy. Millions have lost their jobs. Travel, tourism and the hospitality industry have wound down to a halt. Small businesses everywhere have closed down. Many people have had to take a salary cut. Migrant labour wove a poignant thread over the country as they left behind the big cities in which they earned a living and set out on foot for their homes hundreds and thousands of miles away, since all transportation had shut during the lockdown. Their epic and enormously tragic journeys across the country with little food, water and money is an indelible stain upon the national conscience.

Meanwhile, free of man's destructive influence, all of nature has been blooming. The skies are dawning softly blue (except in the monsoons). Spring and summer have unfolded across the world with flowers blooming, birds singing and trees bearing flowers and fruits. Wild animals have ventured into cities. Dolphins were spotted in Venice and a deer crashed into a Mumbai slum. Jackals wandered freely in Tel Aviv and a pelican landed at St James Park, London. Pollution across the world has skydived because factories were closed for months and the roads remain empty. For the first time in centuries, business came to a halt and the weary earth has begun to heal.

As I write this almost four months after the lockdown was imposed, some of the countries have lifted their lockdowns, including parts of India. However, the virus continues to cut a swathe across the world and the count of the sick and the dying is mounting. And the future? It's anybody's guess.

So here's mine. The Coronavirus has done what no one on earth was able to do. Got the world to stop in its tracks. To pause. And a pause is a creative thing. It is when we pause that we allow our minds to rest and for new things to enter our consciousness. So, could it be that the virus is actually helping sweep clean the old world and bring about a new one?

The economy is down on its knees across the world. It is not impossible to conceive of it disintegrating altogether. Even though its collapse is causing immense suffering, it would have happened sooner or later, for we cannot sustain an economy based on infinite growth in a finite planet. And the cost to the environment, including other species as well as to human society, has been absolutely punitive. Greed has reached a crescendo all over the planet, which has also led to mountains of waste being dumped everywhere. People are on an insatiable quest for more and more, tiring quickly of what they have as they reach out like fretful babies for the next toy.

There are many things we will have to let go of as we move forward towards a saner world. First, we will have to redefine capitalism. It can no longer operate from the profit motive because that converts it into a juggernaut of destruction. Instead, we need to substitute it with the service motive, where entrepreneurs and businesses come up with services and products that can help serve society, and charge a fair but not exploitative price for it. With the end of the profit motive, some of the unwise principles that came along with it such as the compulsion to spend and not save that converted us into consumer junkies will grind to a halt, as well as the concept of using and throwing, just so the wheels of industry could keep spinning at an ever faster pace. Inbuilt obsolescence, another unscrupulous principle, will also mercifully come to an end. The economy will cease to be at the heart of human enterprise as it is today. Instead, serving life will be seen as the highest priority. Personal growth, cultivating relationships, practising arts and crafts, farming, gardening, healing, mentoring, caregiving, nurturing, educating and ethical business, will be various ways of doing this. All livelihoods will be evaluated on the basis of whether they serve life. Those that don't will soon go bankrupt for lack of customers. The highly conscious consumer will choose to serve his own life through his purchasing choices.

Oneness will be the central plank of this emerging world and will govern all operations and systems. Politics, economics, education, medicine, architecture and everything will revolve around the fulcrum of interconnection.

Recognising our innate kinship may be one step towards creating the One-World family that the Indian rishis often talked about. People will gradually recognise the futility of going against the larger good through anti-social and unethical activities because, in an interconnected world, our good is inextricably linked to the larger good. In a world of Oneness there is no other. There is only us.

Today, during the lockdown, most of us are experiencing a life that is rugged in its simplicity. All cars, jewellery and fancy clothing have been locked out of sight. Dressed in home clothes, we spend on nothing much more than food, medicines, household bills and maybe a few more items. No eating out or going out to watch a movie. No travel. No weekend getaways in our second or third homes. Instead of fretting and fuming, many are finding this freedom from frenetic activity and consumption to be a great relief.

Thanks to the lack of domestic help, most of us are learning vital lessons in self-reliance as we take responsibility for running our houses on our own with the help of other family members. Work-from-home is finally integrating our lives. Instead of work and home being at two ends of the spectrum, linked only through a lengthy commute, we saunter from our bedroom to our living room and, presto, we are at work. Or vice versa.

With migrant labour returning to their villages, maybe the time has come for the development of villages into sturdy and independent units that do not require its inhabitants to trek to the cities in order to earn a livelihood. Urban sprawls will be arrested and cities may shrink as people look for greener and cleaner spaces. As a follower of Mahatma Gandhi, I am hoping that his dream of Panchayati Raj will come into being.

Could it be that we are being trained to leave behind the world of materialism and enter into a harder, physically more demanding but, ultimately, healthier, more harmonious and happier world? Could we be making the shift from Kaliyug to Satyug? Even if the Coronavirus does not bring about all the change, my guess is that it is a very significant step forward.

Acknowledgements

My infinite love and gratitude to the Source for everything, but especially for the spiritual awakening that set me on the path of spirituality and made me who I am.

My fervent gratitude to my parents, Atyaril Koshy Varughese and Aleykutty Varughese for having given me life, and for modeling love, selflessness, honesty and an incorruptible value system. Love you both forever.

I cannot forget my five sisters, Mariamma, Molly, Leela, Susan and Sheela who have made my life journey so joyous, and loved me unconditionally even when I felt unlovable.

Deep gratitude also goes to my publisher at *Life Positive*, Aditya Ahluwalia, for having been an excellent boss, and for having given me the opportunity to be part of *Life Positive* for so many years.

My homage to my mentors, a few living, many more on the other shore: my former publisher Nari Hira, Eckhart Tolle, J. Krishnamurti, Dada Vaswani, Mahatma Gandhi, Jesus Christ, the Buddha and Sri Krishna, all of whom have influenced me profoundly.

My love and gratitude to Sr Shivani, such a lighthouse of wisdom, for graciously writing the beautiful foreword.

Deep gratitude to Devdutt Patnaik, Shobhaa De, Maa Gyaan Suveera, Sadhvi Bhagwati and Swami Tejomayanda for their generous words at the back of the book.

Profound thanks to Hay House and Ashok Chopra, for agreeing to publish my book. Love and gratitude to former editor-in-chief Ruchita Ahuja for her masterful editing of the book and her co-operative and encouraging attitude.

And, finally, thanks to you, dear reader, for picking up this book. I pray that it will comfort you in moments of sorrow or loss, inspire you when discouraged and ignite hope in this human adventure. May it support you in becoming the best you can be.